What people are say

A Life Worth L

William Ferraiolo's new book, *A Life Worth Living: Meditations On God, Death and Stoicism*, represents an essential contribution to all who struggle with living a meaningful life. The counsel and alternative perspectives offered are practical, pragmatic, and comforting. Life has a way of delivering hardship of one form or another to all, but the suffering that typically follows is often unnecessary. Using Ferraiolo's guidance, one gains the frame of reference that minimizes the hardships in life while maximizing the many wonderful and miraculous opportunities that come from living.

I have highly recommended Ferraiolo's earlier book, *Meditations on Self-Discipline and Failure*, but I think his new work is even better. Don't miss a chance to gain a new personal freedom – be sure to read *A Life Worth Living: Meditations On God, Death and Stoicism*!

Eldon Taylor, PhD, *New York Times* best-selling author of *Choices and Illusions*, host of the *Provocative Enlightenment Radio Show*

I loved this book, *A Life Worth Living: Meditations on God, Death and Stoicism*, a no-nonsense read depicting just what it takes to apply Stoicism in life fearlessly. Powerful and empowering!
George Bradley, author of *A Better Human: The Stoic Heart, Mind, and Soul*

"How should we live?" "What is a good life?" These questions are as relevant today as they were in Ancient Greece or the cosmopolis of the Roman Empire. The rapid pace of change in contemporary life leaves all of us struggling to make sense of who we are, and how to be happy. William Ferraiolo's new book, *A Life Worth Living: Meditations on God, Death and Stoicism*, is a serious contribution to the contemporary struggle to answer timeless questions. Rigorous but accessible, Ferraiolo's essays will challenge both the professional philosopher as well as persons from all walks of life who think seriously about the value of their lives. Like his earlier work, *Meditations on Self-Discipline and Failure: Stoic Exercise for Mental Fitness*, Ferraiolo's new work represents a successful attempt to adapt classical Stoic Philosophy to the 21st Century in an accessible idiom unique to all his work.

Dr. Barry F. Vaughan, philosopher, Mesa College

I am the host of a podcast named Stoic Mettle, which focuses on making the philosophy of Stoicism accessible to laymen. I had William on my podcast to discuss his book, Meditations on Self-Discipline and Failure. In a space where so many people are keen to show off their intellectual prowess, babbling on about esoteric ideas, I was pleasantly surprised by William's down-to-earth way of approaching the subject. It was a refreshing way of thinking about old ideas. The podcast we did together was well received by my audience, and is still one of my most downloaded shows as well as a personal favorite of mine. People who are interested in Stoicism should read his new book, *A Life Worth Living: Meditations on God, Death and Stoicism*.

Scott Hebert, host of the *Stoic Mettle* podcast

Bill Ferraiolo's new book, *A Life Worth Living: Meditations on God, Death and Stoicism*, like his two previous volumes, is an earnest, erudite, yet accessible celebration of classical wisdom and common sense, with renewed emphasis on the path to equanimity in the face of the inevitable. Those of us who are about to die salute him!

Phil Hutcheon, author of *Nobody Roots for Goliath* and *Where Triples Go To Die*

In these chaotic times I always look for fresh perspectives to help reframe my and my patients' worldview. In this case the philosophy may not be fresh, but the perspective certainly is. Dr. Ferraiolo makes Stoicism tangible as he offers meditations on its applicability to anxiety, grief, relationships, and God. This wisdom mixed in with enjoyable examinations on No Country for Old Men and other asides makes this work something I'll return to again and again.

Ryan Engelstad, host of *The Best Medicine* podcast

A Life Worth Living

Meditations on God, Death
and Stoicism

A Life Worth Living

Meditations on God, Death and Stoicism

William Ferraiolo

BOOKS

Winchester, UK
Washington, USA

JOHN HUNT PUBLISHING

First published by O-Books, 2020
O-Books is an imprint of John Hunt Publishing Ltd., 3 East St., Alresford,
Hampshire SO24 9EE, UK
office@jhpbooks.com
www.johnhuntpublishing.com
www.o-books.com

For distributor details and how to order please visit the 'Ordering' section on our website.

ISBN: 978 1 78904 304 4
978 1 78904 305 1 (ebook)
Library of Congress Control Number: 2018962202

A CIP catalogue record for this book is available from the British Library.

Design: Stuart Davies

UK: Printed and bound by CPI Group (UK) Ltd, Croydon, CR0 4YY
US: Printed and bound by Thomson-Shore, 7300 West Joy Road, Dexter, MI 48130

We operate a distinctive and ethical publishing philosophy in
all areas of our business, from our global network of authors to
production and worldwide distribution.

Contents

For the Ferraiolo, Robison, and Garcia clans

Acknowledgements

This book would not exist without the diligent efforts of the wonderful staff at John Hunt Publishing. I am very grateful to all of them, and I would not wish to leave anyone out. So, thank you all! Finally, my wife, Jennifer Ferraiolo, is my inspiration in all things, and the most indispensable person in my life. All gratitude begins and ends with my Jenny.

Introduction

This is a collection of ruminations about Stoic philosophy, the existence and nature of God, the inevitability of mortality, and other elements of the human condition. Most of the book you are holding has taken shape gradually over that last two decades of writing, research, classroom teaching, academic conference participation, and life experiences to which most readers will relate quite readily because they are fairly universal. There is nothing particularly special or unique about the author. Indeed, quite the reverse has been asserted on many occasions – and not without reason. Each of us is a small, ephemeral, and insignificant element of the vast universe, and yet – we *are* here! Life presents itself for the living.

The world is a rough place and no one gets out alive. Our time here is limited – and we do not know how much time any of us is allotted. We are *entitled* to precisely *none* of it. None of us *had* to be born. The universe did not have to be anthropic (i.e. habitable by creatures like us). Indeed, the probability of human life evolving in any universe of the infinitely many universes that could have been (or, perhaps, that there *are*) appears to be vanishingly small. Our existence as a species, and our presence here as individuals, is either literally a miracle, or it is the statistical approximation of the miraculous. Human life, as difficult as it often is, as emotionally challenging as it can be, and as ubiquitously destined to culminate in death as it appears to be, is still an astonishing gift – and appears to be preferable to the alternative (for most of us). Thus, as Socrates declared during the trial that led to his execution, we should recognize that "the unexamined life is not worth living." As reasoning beings, we are obligated to train that unique faculty on the lives we are living, the choices we are making, and upon our understanding of the world in which we find ourselves embedded. This book is one author's attempt to understand a few central elements of the human condition. This is life examined – albeit imperfectly and very incompletely. Let us hope that life is, indeed, worth living. The author hopes that this book is worth reading. There is, of course, only one reliable way for the reader to find out. Good luck, and thank you for giving this work a chance. Enjoy.

The IDEA Method: Stoic Counsel

The condition and characteristic of a philosopher is that he looks to himself for all help or harm.
– Epictetus [*Enchiridion*, 48]

Make your rules of life brief, yet so as to embrace the fundamentals; recurrence to them will then suffice to remove all vexation, and send you back without fretting to the duties to which you must return.
– Marcus Aurelius [*Meditations*, Book Four, 3]

Epictetus was born a slave. Marcus Aurelius became an emperor. Both were Stoics, and adhered to the same root principles of self-discipline, broadly sharing an understanding of the human condition. Here, I present, in skeletal outline, a simple program of personal governance derived from Roman Stoicism as espoused by Epictetus and Marcus Aurelius. What I have dubbed "The IDEA Method" is my attempt to resuscitate a few central tenets of Stoic counsel and to explain and defend their efficacy for responding rationally and effectively to the many vicissitudes and challenges endemic to the human condition. I hope to breathe a bit of new life into a Stoic analysis of self-disciplinary propriety that served the needs of a slave, an emperor, and innumerable lives lived between those two material extremes.

Epictetus spent much of his early life as another man's property and, apparently, sustained a permanent disability resulting from punishment inflicted upon him by his owner. He nonetheless managed to become an influential and highly regarded instructor in the art of living well and maintaining equanimity irrespective of circumstance. Roman culture was influenced, in many respects, by the Stoic worldview and its practical counsel regarding rational and skillful management of common trials. Marcus Aurelius later carried Stoicism to the pinnacle of Roman power, becoming Emperor in the middle of the second century CE. His *Meditations*, intended primarily as a journal for his own reflection and personal edification, was posthumously published and has served as a reliable source of inspiration with its simple instructions for maintaining dignified calm and living a rationally disciplined life. Emperor and slave, it seems, drew strength from the same wellspring.

It is my contention that Stoic counsel may serve just as effectively today as it did nearly two thousand years ago. Material and scientific advancements notwithstanding, the human condition has not changed a great deal during the millennia separating our era from Roman antiquity. We must still make our way within a world that lies almost entirely beyond our control. We must still face death, deprivation, and bodily frailty, as well as events and persons that do not conform to common hopes and expectations. We are still relatively small, and the world is still large and mostly heedless of our concerns. How may one hope to pursue "the good life" in the face of such challenges? What is the starting place from which Stoic counsel offers guidance?

I: Identify the Real Issue

Our troubles often stem from the fact that we desire what we do not have, or are averse to what befalls us. We must recognize the emotional and psychological centrality of our ability to deal rationally with desire and aversion. Failure of proper self-regulation in this arena is a common source of much of our distress and dissatisfaction. Epictetus reminds his students to:

> Remember that desire demands the attainment of that of which you are desirous; and aversion demands the avoidance of that to which you are averse; that he who fails of the object

of his desires is disappointed; and he who incurs the object of his aversion is wretched. [*Enchiridion*, 2]

When we are dissatisfied, it is typically a poor "fit" between our desires and the unfolding of events that causes our distress. We want what is not so. The facts, in and of themselves, are neither good nor bad, but one's attitude toward the facts may cause them to appear fearsome. Epictetus contends:

Men are disturbed not by things, but by the views which they take of things... When, therefore, we are hindered, or disturbed, or grieved, let us never blame anyone but ourselves; that is, our own judgments. [*Enchiridion*, 5]

Perturbation results from our evaluation of conditions or states of affairs with which we are confronted. Desire and aversion color our encounter with "things" as they are.

Sometimes our dissatisfaction arises in response to conditions that are not especially subtle or complex. What, for example, is typically the problem presented by a broken leg? This is (at least in most instances) a diagnostically straightforward matter. The injury causes pain and various forms of temporary disability to which the injured party is generally averse. Although a variety of psychological, spiritual, or even philosophical concerns may, in some cases, arise from the injury and surrounding circumstances (e.g. it is perceived as punishment for some prior moral transgression, or as yet another absurdity confirming the meaninglessness of life, etc.), typically the unpleasantness is efficiently dissipated with time and proper medical attention. If this were the only sort of problem that people experienced, then the market for practical philosophy, as well as most other forms of talk therapy, counselling, and consultation would be far smaller than it is – and philosophical practitioners would be of relatively little use.

5

Much of our distress, both individually and collectively, is not amenable to medical intervention, and time does not appear actually to heal *all* wounds or solve all problems (unless, of course, all problems are, as Stalin quipped, solved by death – and who wants to wait for that "solution"?). One common type of challenge may involve, for instance, an extremely annoying colleague or supervisor with whom one's job requires one to interact on a daily basis. Distress may result from an absence of love or any semblance of affection in one's marriage, and it may be clear to both parties that they dislike being married to each other. In each case, desire and expectation are at loggerheads with one's actual experience of conditions as they stand.

In other circumstances, of course, the real issue may be more difficult to identify or to articulate. A failure of rigorous, careful introspection can occlude the true origin and etiology of our displeasure. When we do not know our own minds and proclivities, we may be unable to discover why sleep does not come easily, or why a career no longer seems fulfilling, or why the general sense of dissatisfaction will not lift, or anxiety will not pass into peace and calm. If the Stoics are right, the "something" that is wrong will, upon careful introspection, prove to be a matter of our attitudes, beliefs, desires, aversions – in short, a matter of dysfunctional *ideas* (broadly construed). It is, therefore, advisable, the Stoics teach us, to "turn inward" and investigate the objects of our desire and aversion if we are to find the real source of our discontent.

D: Distinguish "Internals" from "Externals"

Very little of the world is ours to control. We do not have the power to govern, merely by the exertion of our will, any of the following: the past, the laws of nature, other people (their beliefs, desires, behavior, etc.), political matters, social trends, economic phenomena, the condition of our bodies, and just about everything else that does not directly conform to our decisions, desires, mental efforts – in short, everything that we cannot directly produce by simply deciding or willing that it shall be so. If, on the contrary, one's will can, without assistance or mediation, create a certain state of affairs or cause something to happen, then that state of affairs is directly within one's control. Such matters are, in Epictetan terms, "properly our own affairs." Let us refer to those events and phenomena that directly conform to the agent's will as "internals" and all those that do not as "externals." Epictetan counsel is founded upon this crucial distinction:

> There are things which are within our power, and there are things which are beyond our power. Within our power are opinion, aim, desire, aversion, and, in one word, whatever affairs are our own. Beyond our power are body, property, reputation, office, and, in one word, whatever are not properly our own affairs. [*Enchiridion*, I]

In any circumstance, given any form of distress or unease, it is essential that the distressed person, the sufferer, correctly identify those elements of the circumstance that lie beyond his control (the externals) and distinguish them from those that are within his power (the internals). Failure to correctly distinguish internals from externals, and regulate desire accordingly, virtually ensures frustration, anxiety, and distress.

Consider, for example, a marriage that has ceased to satisfy one or both spouses. The husband's desires, aversions, expectations and, to a large extent at least, his behavior are his to control. His wife's desires, aversions, beliefs, attitudes, and behavior are not. Certainly, he may speak to his wife and engage in other forms of interaction by which he might sway her opinion and causally influence her feelings and subsequent behavior, but note that only his attitudes *directly* conform to his will, while hers require her cooperation, and other intermediate factors (e.g. some means of communication). In such a case, the wise husband will understand that self-improvement, as a man and a spouse, lies within his direct power, whereas the improvement or alteration of his wife's internal and external condition does not. Psychological and emotional dependence upon states of affairs conforming to antecedent hopes or expectations leaves the agent's well-being at the mercy of an often-recalcitrant world. Obviously, the same principle applies *mutatis mutandis* with respect to the wife's relationship to her husband's thoughts and actions (or, for that matter, to her child, coworker, sibling, etc.). With respect to interpersonal relations in general, Marcus Aurelius' *Meditations* provides the following reminder:

> You will not easily find a man coming to grief through indifference to the workings of another's soul; but for those who pay no heed to the motions of their own, unhappiness is their sure reward. [Book Two, 8]

The wise seek to know their own minds so that they may better govern themselves, and do not pin their contentment to winning the hearts and minds of others. The Stoic sage does not make demands on the external world, but instead develops self-discipline so as to deal reasonably with the world as it presents itself.

E: Exert Effort Only Where it can be Effective

It is unwise, unhealthy, and wasteful to expend energy trying to control or to change circumstances that lie beyond one's control and one's ability to enact change. When we bend our efforts on conditions lying beyond our control, we invite disappointment and discontent. Externals *may* conform to our preexisting hopes, but if this occurs, it occurs fortuitously and we cannot depend upon sustained good fortune. Attachments to external objects of desire and aversion open the door to dissatisfaction. Our loved ones, for example, will be taken from us – either when they die, when we die, or due to some event that separates us prior to death. Our bodies and our health will eventually fail, as none of us is immortal. Our accumulated material wealth and goods will be separated from us and, in the long run, will cease even to pass into the hands of those whom we have chosen to receive them. Who today possesses the wealth of Croesus? Who possesses the fruits of Alexander's conquests? Wealth and power are ephemeral. Fame, for those few who attain it, lasts but a moment. Our names will cease to be remembered or uttered. For most of us, this will happen fairly soon after we depart this world. Even the "immortals," however, will eventually be forgotten. Who will remember today's celebrities a thousand years from now? Who will be left to remember them when the human race has passed away and the inexorable law of entropy has rendered the universe uninhabitable? In the long, long run, we all face the same future of extinction and disappearance without a trace. In his *Meditations*, Marcus Aurelius nicely articulates the point:

> Our mental powers should enable us to perceive the swiftness with which all things vanish away: their bodies in the world of space, and their remembrance in the world of time. [Book Two, 12]

It is, therefore, unhealthy to become attached to anything or any state of affairs that belongs to the external world's dispensations – for such things do not truly belong to us and will be lost to us eventually.

The wise understand this and do not waste time and effort trying to command anything that does not answer to their commands. They do not desire that external states of affairs should be one way as opposed to another. Instead, they focus their desire only on objects that they can direct by the force of their will alone. The administration of the external world is not up to us, but each rational agent has the power to administer his own desires, aversions, and attitudes *about* the world and its unfolding. Those whose desires and aversions attach only to matters that lie within their control do not see their desires go unsatisfied and do not experience anything to which they are averse. One who desires something that he has the power to produce simply produces it. One who is only averse to that which he has the direct power to avoid simply avoids the undesirable by the force of his own will. If, for example, one is averse to becoming a liar, and one has properly disciplined oneself in matters of honesty, then one simply does not lie and, thereby, unerringly avoids the object of aversion. One who desires a tranquil mind, and disciplines himself to maintain tranquility irrespective of circumstance, thereby attains what he desires and can fail to obtain it only through inadequate self-control. As Epictetus reminds us in "Concerning Naso":

> So, in our own case, we take it to be the work of one who studies philosophy to bring his will into harmony with events; so that none of the things which happen may happen against our inclination, nor those which do not happen be desired by us. Hence they who have settled this point have it in their power never to be disappointed in what they seek, nor to incur what they shun; but to lead their own lives without sorrow, fear, or perturbation, and in society to preserve all the natural or acquired relations of son, father, brother, citizen, husband, wife, neighbor, fellow traveler, ruler, or subject. Something like this is what we take to be the work of a philosopher. [*Discourses*, p. 122]

The practical philosopher points the way to a sustained equanimity that, for the disciplined practitioner, survives the slings and arrows of fortune.

A: Accept the Rest – *Amor Fati*

The world is as it is and is not as it otherwise might have been. When we resist or reject the world as it stands and struggle against it, the world always has its way. This is so because the external world is not ours to control and need not respond to our demands or conform to our desires. We should, therefore, make no attempt to command anything but ourselves. All else is best embraced as an expression of what the Stoics regarded as God's will or, for those skeptical of intelligent design or guidance, manifestations of the natural laws that allow for a habitable world. Epictetus calls our attention to the benefits of a well-regulated attitude concerning external conditions:

> Demand not that events should happen as you wish; but wish them to happen as they do happen and your life will be serene. [*Enchiridion*, 8]

It is this attitude – this *amor fati* – that, centuries later, Nietzsche regarded as the primary expression of the noble character. In *Ecce Homo*, under the heading "Why I Am So Clever," he states:

> My formula for what is great in mankind is *amor fati*: not to wish for anything other than that which is; whether behind, ahead, or for all eternity. Not just to put up with the inevitable – much less to hide it from oneself, for all idealism is lying to oneself in the face of the necessary – but to love it. [II, 10]

Nietzsche himself was not exactly a Stoic, and the Stoics did not explicitly use the expression "*amor fati*," but their respective worldviews dovetail nicely on at least this one bit of counsel concerning the nature of a good life. The wise have no complaint against the universe. They have learned to love the world as it is, and have embraced their fate within the grand, unfolding evolution all around them. It is, as Nietzsche might say, noble to love one's life and the chance to experience challenges as they arise. We see in Nietzsche's remark an echo of Epictetus' advice to his students:

> Fix your desire and aversion on riches or poverty; the one will be disappointed, the other incurred. Fix them on health, power, honors, your country, friends, children – in short, on anything beyond the control of your will – you will be unfortunate. But fix them on Zeus, on the gods; give yourself up to these; let these govern; let your powers be ranged on the same side with these, and how can you be troubled any longer? But if, poor wretch, you envy, and pity, and are jealous, and tremble, and never cease a single day from complaining of yourself and the gods, why do you boast of your education? [*Discourses*, p. 135]

Those who use their intellect and other skills in the attempt to acquire and hold material possessions, or fame, or power over others, thereby betray their ignorance of this crucial matter of discernment. One who contends against the world or insists upon controlling it fights a losing and foolish battle. The world itself does not need to suit our whims. We must condition ourselves to love life in the world as we find it.

Conclusion

The Stoics have provided a template for contending with the many exigencies and challenges of the human condition. I have presented the bare outlines of a method by which some central Stoic insights regarding rational self-governance may be applied to the kinds of adversity that Epictetus and Marcus Aurelius addressed and that still confront us today. The full Stoic worldview involves much more, obviously, than those few maxims or guiding platitudes herein explored. The center of practical gravity is, however, expressible in a few fundamental principles. As a handy mnemonic device, I have labeled this central bit of Stoic counsel the "IDEA Method" to indicate the decision procedure by which some Stoic wisdom may be applied to various common difficulties with which we all too frequently struggle:

I: Identify the Real Issue

D: Distinguish "Internals" from "Externals"

E: Exert Effort Only Where it can be Effective

A: Accept the Rest – *Amor Fati*

How much needless suffering might be obviated by the diligent application of this simple but powerful counsel? Stoicism, I claim, offers tools by which reason may sustain us in rationally grounded equanimity, even in a seemingly harsh and indifferent world.

Stoic Anxiolytics

When I see anyone anxious, I say, what does this man want? Unless he wanted something or other not in his power, how could he still be anxious?
– Epictetus [*Discourses*, Book II, Ch. 13]

O the consolation of being able to thrust aside and cast into oblivion every tiresome intrusive impression, and in a trice be utterly at peace!
– Marcus Aurelius [*Meditations*, Book Five, 2]

Anxiety Disorders affect about 40 million American adults age 18 years and older (about 18%) in a given year, causing them to be filled with fearfulness and uncertainty.
– National Institute of Mental Health (2009)

Anxiety, whatever else it may involve, seems always to hinge upon the possibility that some desire may be frustrated or some aversion incurred. Anxiety, therefore, arises as a result of the relationship between one's mental states and the (actual or perceived) possibility that conditions will not produce the desiderata of those states. In short, we experience anxiety because things may not turn out as we wish. Perhaps the problem is not located in the unfolding of events, but rather in the nature of the wishing. I will argue that the Roman Stoics correctly analyzed the necessary conditions for the arising of anxiety, and offered an effective prescription for the treatment and prevention of this disordered emotional state – a prescription that does not involve benzodiazepines such as Valium or Xanax, but one that holds out the promise of more stable and enduring anxiolytic effect than synthetic antianxiety medications can plausibly offer. Ultimately, anxiety can afflict only those whose desires are not rationally governed. There is little that anyone can do about the vicissitudes of the external world and the unraveling of events therein, but there is a great deal that a rational agent can do to manage the objects and direction of desire and aversion. Since they are not dispensed in tablet or capsule form, Stoic anxiolytics remain available without prescription and exhibit an extraordinarily benign side effect profile. They rarely cause weight gain, sexual dysfunction, or uncontrollable movements of the limbs. Physiological dependence is relatively uncommon – and not especially pernicious. Instead, Stoicism offers rationally grounded, proven psychological techniques for the gradual development of consistent self-mastery and emotional detachment from those elements of the human condition that tend to cause the most pervasive and unsettling forms of fear, anxiety, and avoidable disquiet.

Modern Pandemic, Ancient Therapy

In *Coping with Anxiety*, Edmund Bourne and Lorna Garano note the prevalence of anxiety in contemporary Western culture, and explain various non-pharmacological strategies for addressing anxiety disorders and their various manifestations (while noting that some cases of severe anxiety may require – or at least benefit significantly from – pharmaceutical intervention so as to reduce biochemical obstacles to other forms of therapeutic management of the disorder). The authors remind the reader of the multifaceted nature of anxiety as a psychiatric and physiological dysfunction, detail many of the most common symptoms, and note the corresponding need to address the syndrome on several fronts:

> The fact that anxiety can affect you on physiological, behavioral, and psychological levels has important implications for your attempts to cope. A complete program of coping with anxiety must address all three components.

You need to learn how to reduce physiological reactivity, eliminate avoidance behavior, and change self-talk that perpetuates a state of apprehension and worry. [2003, p. 2]

Anxiety may be on the increase in the contemporary industrialized world, but it is certainly nothing new. The Roman Stoics could not have addressed the physiological impact of neurotransmitters such as serotonin, dopamine, norepinephrine, or GABA and, obviously, could not entertain chemical anxiolytics or antidepressants as methods of intervention. They could only hope to address cognition and behavior in their attempts to manage and/or overcome anxiety and its sometimes debilitating effects. Though they were typically on offer in oral form, Stoic anxiolytics could not be ingested as pills or elixirs. From this, however, it does not follow that their methods of therapeutic intervention were inefficacious. In fact, it is not at all clear that modern forms of talk therapy have advanced any appreciable distance from the counsels of Stoic wise men such as Seneca, Epictetus, and Marcus Aurelius. Many of the various forms of contemporary cognitive behavioral therapy are little more than peripherally modified counsel derived from an essentially Stoic foundation – perhaps best encapsulated in Epictetus' advice that each of us should:

Demand not that events should happen as you wish; but wish them to happen as they do happen and your life will be serene. [*Enchiridion*, 8]

The Stoic master, and former slave, thereby indicates that serenity is not attained by attempts to order events in the external world so as to satisfy one's preexisting or stubbornly-held desires (as most external events are quite clearly beyond any agent's control), but rather that serenity ensues from a rational ordering of desires and aversions (i.e. a proper governance of "wishing") so as to embrace and attune the will to that which it lacks the power to impose by fiat or determine without assistance or mediation from external powers. In other words, tranquility results from a rationally disciplined will whereas anxiety results from failures of self-discipline and a refusal to restrict desire and aversion to that sphere within which the agent's will is determinative. What is needed then is a method of rational, effective self-governance and a means of bringing desire and aversion under the control of well-tutored and judiciously applied reason. This is the heart of Stoic counsel and, ultimately, the centerpiece of modern talk-therapeutic treatments for anxiety, depression, and other forms of psychophysical dysfunction.

Stoic Foundation of Contemporary Talk Therapy

In a letter to Nero's police commissioner, Serenus, who is afflicted with a nervous disorder, Seneca counsels that:

> We must learn to strengthen self-restraint, curb luxury, temper ambition, moderate anger, view poverty calmly, cultivate frugality (though many are ashamed of it), use readily available remedies for natural desires, keep restive aspirations and a mind intent upon the future under lock and key, and make it our business to get our riches from ourselves rather than from Fortune. ["On Tranquility," p. 91]

By "Fortune," Seneca means to refer to all that lies beyond the will's control. All desire and aversion concerning the dispensations of Fortune are in need of "remedies" derived from a cultivated and strengthened "self-restraint." In this way, "riches" (i.e. tranquility and equanimity) are garnered from relinquishing irrational attachments to any external conditions that do not conform to the dictates of the will.

Albert Ellis, the father of Rational Emotive Behavior Therapy (REBT), explicitly credits the Roman Stoics with providing the foundation for his very successful and popular brand of cognitive intervention. In his best-selling manual of guided self-governance, *A Guide to Rational Living*, the chapter entitled "Conquering Anxiety and Panic" offers this advice regarding attachment to conditions beyond one's control:

> Try not to exaggerate the importance or significance of things. Your favorite cup, as Epictetus noted many centuries ago, merely represents a cup that you like. Your wife and children, however delightful, remain mortals... But if you exaggeratedly convince yourself that this is the *only* cup in the world or that your life would be completely empty without your wife and children, you will overestimate their value and make yourself needlessly vulnerable to their possible loss. [1997, p. 174]

It is possible (and, in fact, quite healthy) to simultaneously love one's spouse and children while also recognizing that their health, well-being, and survival are beyond one's direct control. There is no benefit in obsessing about their mortality and their unavoidable human frailties. There is, however, great benefit in directing one's mental energies toward enjoying family and friends, treating them properly, and loving them as deeply as possible – exerting maximum effort to be a virtuous spouse and parent (as such *efforts* lie within one's power). Desiring that loved ones should *always* be happy and healthy virtually assures frustration, anxiety, and disappointment, as few mortals manage perpetual happiness (and *all* eventually die). Desiring, however, to *try one's best* to support, assist, and enhance the beloved's well-being (recognizing that the actual attainment of that well-being is beyond one's direct power), leaves far less potential for anxiety and debilitating worry. If the desire is to be gentle, honest, compassionate, etc., then the only ground for anxiety in the matter is concern about failures of self-discipline and/or behaviors that fail to accord with reason. This anxiety may be assuaged and should diminish as continued practice enhances one's willpower and rectitude. If desire is permitted to extend beyond the sphere of those conditions lying within the power of one's unmediated will, then anxiety is invited to wreak havoc upon oneself and, indirectly, upon the lives of others.

Death Anxiety

Aversions cause anxiety insofar as the conditions to which one is averse seem possible or probable. Anxiety concerning death is, not surprisingly, fairly pervasive because everyone knows that death is inescapable. If, however, one can psychologically embrace the ineradicable fact that we are (both individually and collectively) headed for extinction, or at least regard this fact with detached, rational indifference, then death anxiety cannot easily take hold. It is only aversion to death, and the prospect of incurring that aversion, that produces anxiety in the face of our limited stay in the world. The Roman Emperor, and Stoic practitioner, Marcus Aurelius understood the full implications of death's inevitability and universality. He enjoined himself to:

Remind yourself constantly of all the physicians, now dead, who used to knit their brows over their ailing patients; of all the astrologers who so solemnly predicted their clients' doom; the philosophers who expatiated so endlessly on death or immortality; the great commanders who slew their thousands; the despots who wielded powers of life and death with such terrible arrogance, as if themselves were gods who could never die; the whole cities which have perished completely, Helice, Pompeii, Herculaneum, and others without number. After that, recall one by one each of your own acquaintances; how one buried another, only to be laid low himself and buried in turn by a third, and all in so brief a space of time. Observe, in short, how transient and trivial is all mortal life; yesterday a drop of semen, tomorrow a handful of spice or ashes. Spend, therefore, these fleeting moments on earth as Nature would have you spend them, and then go to your rest with good grace, as an olive falls in its season, with a blessing for the earth that bore it and a thanksgiving to the tree that gave it life. [*Meditations*, Book Four, 48]

Death itself is no evil and no legitimate source of anxiety. It is only a foolish desire for immortality that causes our irrational resistance to the inevitable.

In his contemporary best-seller, *The Feeling Good Handbook*, David Burns suggests a rational cognitive restructuring of distorted, unjustifiable fears about death as the ultimate and most terrifying unknown confronting humankind. His suggested methods of rational restructuring could easily have been lifted from the pages of the Roman Stoic masters who recognized that death is either not experienced (by the dead), or is experienced merely as a transition from one phase of existence to the next:

> Death will either be "something" or "nothing." If it's "something" it won't be "unknown" and if it's "nothing," there will be "nothing" to worry about! [1989, p. 265]

The cessation of one's existence cannot engender legitimate fear – as one must exist in order to suffer or be harmed in any way. If death ends us, then it *a fortiori* ends our troubles as well. If death is not the cessation of one's existence, then it is nothing more than the continuation of life in some new form. We have all undergone numerous transformations throughout our lifetimes, and there is no obvious justification for unique anxiety surrounding death as merely one more transformation. Moreover, the world has seen innumerable lives come and go, and Epictetus reminds us that nothing of any great moment is lost when nature reclaims what it has given us on loan:

"But it is now time to die." Why do you say die? Do not talk of the thing in tragic strain; but state the thing as it is, that it is time for your material part to revert whence it came. And where is the terror of this? What part of the world is going to be lost? What is going to happen that is new or prodigious? [*Discourses*, Book IV, Ch. Seven]

Where, indeed, is the source of our terror? Death itself cannot cause our fear, but only the *belief* that death is awful can serve to terrify. We need only relinquish this belief to deprive death of its power to horrify us and generate crippling anxiety.

Why, do you not know, then, that the origin of all human evils, and of baseness and cowardice, is not death, but rather the fear of death? Fortify yourself, therefore, against this. Hither let all your discourses, readings, exercises, tend. And then you will know that only in this way are men made free. [Book III, Ch. 26]

Death cannot be overcome, but the *fear* of death can be mastered. Stoicism holds out the promise of gaining control over one's attitude concerning the inevitability of death.

Performance and Social Anxiety

Another stunningly pervasive source of anxiety is the aversion to failure and/or negative judgment about oneself in the estimation of others. Performance and social anxiety can afflict only those who are averse to poor performance and/or those who regard failure as an external state of affairs to which they are potentially subject. If, on the other hand, one is averse *only* to failures of self-discipline, and remains indifferent to all external conditions and judgments consequent upon one's intellectual or bodily performance, then anxiety can only arise to the extent that the possibility of inadequate self-governance rears its undisciplined head. It is, for example, one thing to have an aversion to being *found out* as an adulterer, but quite another to have an aversion to *being* an adulterer. A man of the former stripe is apt to commit adultery and then suffer the anxiety associated with getting caught (and all the subsequent indignities), whereas a man whose aversion is to *committing* adultery will only have to concern himself with the self-discipline necessary to resist temptation. If he is successful in this matter, then there can be no fear of getting caught. One might still experience anxiety concerning a false *accusation* of infidelity, but only if one fails to disavow attachment to the opinions (especially the *false* opinions) of others can this worry develop any purchase upon one's psychological or emotional stability. Recognizing that the beliefs and opinions of other persons are beyond one's control provides liberation from anxiety stemming from potential disapprobation, attacks upon one's character, etc. Epictetus informs us as to a relevant goal of Stoic training:

> Not to be disappointed in our desire, nor fall into anything which we would avoid. To this ought our training to be directed. For without vigorous and steady training, it is not possible to preserve our desire undisappointed and our aversion unincurred; and therefore, if we allow it to be externally employed on things uncontrollable by will, be assured that your desire will neither gain its object, nor your aversion avoid it. [*Discourses*, Book III, Ch. 12]

So, rigorous training promises liberation from the all-too-common distresses of the poorly disciplined human condition. We need not (and *should* not) concern ourselves with the thoughts, opinions, and behaviors of others. As these are beyond our control, they ought also to lie beyond our concern. Everyone may regard us as a failure or a pathetic creature, but this does not make it so. True success is a matter of making one's best effort, given the circumstances, and is in no way dependent upon external affairs, the approval of others, or even the cooperation of one's own body. When we evaluate only our *efforts*, our exertions of will, and remain indifferent to the consequences thereof (as these are not ours to control), we liberate ourselves from needless distress and subjugation to the winds and whims of capricious fate or the evaluation of our character by other persons. Given his position as Emperor, Marcus Aurelius well understood the peril of pegging one's contentment to the opinions that others might form concerning his character and reminded himself to disregard evaluations of his performance as ruler of the world's mightiest empire:

> You will not easily find a man coming to grief through indifference to the workings of another's soul; but for those who pay no heed to the motions of their own, unhappiness is their sure reward. [*Meditations*, Book Two, 8]

The wise cultivate *self*-rectification and do not permit themselves to be troubled by "the workings of another's soul," because they recognize that such matters are not subject to their will. If we set our intentions on healthy habits of thought and conduct, devoting all our available mental energy to the improvement of ourselves and our engagement with conditions as they present themselves to us, we leave no room for obsession over the way in which we may be perceived or judged by others.

Conclusion

The heart of Stoic counsel regarding anxiety and its various sources is the injunction to carefully distinguish between that which is and that which is not within our control. We can learn to control, to some extent at least, our desires, aversions, pursuits, and interests. If we reason carefully, we can also learn to wisely concern ourselves with *only* those phenomena that conform to the dictates of our will, and to embrace (or at least accept with detached indifference) those phenomena over which our will exerts no authority. Anxiety attaching to matters lying beyond the agent's control is fundamentally irrational, unhealthy, and counterproductive to the project of rational self-governance. It is quite readily avoidable via diligent analysis of the human condition and the limitations circumscribing the sphere within which the human will reigns supreme. The Roman Stoic understanding of anxiety, its causes, its effects, and its treatment, is every bit as applicable and efficacious today as it was roughly two millennia ago. We would do well to heed this wise counsel and offer reverent gratitude for the insights of those ancient Roman sages to whom credit is due.

Stoic Simplicity: The Pursuit of Virtue

The simple person is a person without pretensions, unconcerned with himself, his image or his reputation; he doesn't calculate, has no secrets, and acts without guile, ulterior motives, agendas, or plans. [1996, p. 155]
– André Comte-Sponville

For the Stoic, then, doing philosophy meant practicing how to "live": that is how to live freely... in that we give up desiring that which does not depend on us and is beyond our control... [1995, p. 86]
– Pierre Hadot

Seek not good from without; seek it within yourselves, or you will never find it. [1944, Ch. 25]
– Epictetus

Simplicity is, I shall argue, an indispensable element of the virtuous character. The term "simplicity," and the concept to which it refers, are contextually malleable and indicate different facets of our attitudes, beliefs, practices, theories, designs, etc. depending upon the specific interest at issue. As the Comte-Sponville epigraph at the head of this paper indicates, however, there is a conception of simplicity as a character trait and disposition primarily regarding one's values, intentions, and behavioral tendencies. I intend to address the phenomenon of simplicity insofar as it is constitutive of one's character, and also to argue that it is a cardinal (though often underappreciated) virtue – every bit as fundamental to a well-lived life as is wisdom, compassion, or fortitude. Simplicity, as I will use the term, refers to a disposition in favor of the rational governance of desire and aversion and, in particular, the renunciation of pretense. The simple person eschews interests rooted in concern about the perceptions and attitudes of other persons. Simplicity, in short, is a rational restriction of one's interests to the sphere of one's direct, unmediated control – and a correlative disregard for matters lying beyond that sphere (especially one's "image" or reputation). Historical figures as diverse as the Buddha, Epicurus, Socrates, Diogenes, Epictetus, Marcus Aurelius, Saint Francis, and EF Schumacher have advocated the cultivation of simplicity as a morally and/or prudentially indispensable component of an admirable life. In his contemporary classic, *Voluntary Simplicity*, Duane Elgin (1993) elucidates the core concept of simplicity as it pertains to the art of living:

> To live more simply is to live more purposefully and with a minimum of needless distraction. The particular expression of simplicity is a personal matter. We each know where our lives are unnecessarily complicated. We are all painfully aware of the clutter and pretense that weigh upon us and make our passage through the world more cumbersome and awkward... Simplicity of living means meeting life face-to-face. It means confronting life clearly, without unnecessary distractions. It means being direct and honest in relationships of all kinds. [1993, pp. 24–25]

As an homage to part of the ancient groundwork of this contemporary ethos, I will present and defend the Roman Stoic conception, analysis, and explication of simplicity as a central element of the virtuous character and of a life plan engendering serenity, calm, and equanimity.

Virtue as Cornerstone

The Stoic lifestyle is, at root, the single-minded pursuit of virtue – conceived as life lived in accordance with reason and with a minimum of disingenuous affectation. Virtue is, to some extent at least, an absence of vice. The agent that is innocent of vicious ulterior motives, guile, a hidden agenda, etc., will be largely trustworthy – if for no other reason than disinterest in some of the most common compulsions to mischief. The simple character is devoid of dissimulation, posturing and, perhaps most importantly, the desire to appear to be more accomplished and more impressive, either in the eyes of others or in one's own estimation, than is actually the case. In fact, simplicity entails a disregard for appearances tout court. Appearances, reputation, and social status are detachable from virtue, wisdom, and the project of living a rational, authentic life. Virtue is not founded upon popularity, wealth, or political power. If Socrates was wise, neither the disapprobation of large segments of the Athenian population nor his relative lack of wealth and political power could make him less so. The Cynic, Diogenes, was deemed a madman by many of his contemporaries. This assessment may or may not have had its merits, but the assessment itself did not imbue the homeless, impoverished Diogenes with either vice or virtue. The wise look to themselves for the rectification of their character, and the satisfaction attained thereby, whereas the unenlightened allow their contentment to depend upon the evaluation of others and/or various circumstances unfolding beyond their control (e.g. wealth, power, reputation, etc.). Epictetus uses a stark illustration to distinguish those areas upon which the external world can impinge from those that are psychologically and emotionally beyond its reach:

> But someone takes me by the collar, and drags me to the forum; and then all the rest cry out, "Philosopher, what good do your principles do you? See you are being dragged to prison; see, you are going to lose your head!" And, pray, what rule of philosophy could I contrive, that when a stronger than myself lays hold on my collar, I should not be dragged; or that, when ten men pull me at once, and throw me into prison, I should

not be thrown there? But have I learned nothing then? I have learned to know, whatever happens, that if it concerns not my moral purpose, it is nothing to me. [Epictetus, 1944, Ch. 29]

So, Epictetus informs us that our "moral purpose" (i.e. living a virtuous life in conformity with reason) should be our overriding concern and guiding interest. Our moral purpose is in no way dependent upon the cooperation of other persons, the external world or, indeed, even the obedience or complicity of the body itself. Even a man paralyzed from the neck down can discipline himself to accept his physiological condition with grace and courage, as opposed to bemoaning his disability and cursing his fate. Only the application of rigorous mental discipline is necessary for living a rationally governed life in the face of any challenges that may, and inevitably will, arise. Those who are emotionally mature direct their concern and mental energy to the project of self-rectification and the strengthening of their resolve, as opposed to wasting their limited capacities on needlessly complex schemes designed to appeal to the powerful, appease the masses, or attain the material stuff of ephemeral worldly advantage. The Stoic prizes virtue above any external commodity and does not conflate the former with the latter.

Simplicity and Material Wealth

The Stoic conception of simplicity should not be presumed to necessitate poverty regarding one's material possessions or an absence of political and economic power. Though Stoicism comports nicely with voluntary poverty and political disengagement, it should be noted that these conditions are not prerequisites of Stoic simplicity, nor are they necessary consequences of adopting the Stoic lifestyle. Both Seneca and Marcus Aurelius lived lives of considerable wealth and power while professing adherence to and, by most accounts, living in accordance with root Stoic values. Provided that one does not sacrifice one's virtue or abrogate one's obligation to pursue correct "moral purpose" in the course of any particular attainment, then external accouterments such as wealth, power, fame, physical health, etc. are simply to be regarded with detached indifference and governed with sensible stewardship for as long as they are subject to one's management. When any of these indifferent ephemera pass away (and they all will), the passage should be regarded with detached equanimity and recognized as a simple, natural, and inevitable instance of returning that which is not truly one's own to the dispensations of the external world that briefly endows one with some material advantage or other. Much as one takes care of a rented home or a hotel room with respect for the rightful owner's property, until that property is to be returned and relinquished without distress, similarly one should consider one's own home, body, loved ones, wealth, etc. as mere transient phenomena briefly on loan and subject to reclamation at any moment. Nothing that is not subject to one's own exertion of will ought to be regarded as essential to the instantiation of life in accordance with proper moral purpose. Virtue is internal to the sphere of the agent's direct control. It is a matter of choice and discipline. Any "externals" are, therefore, "indifferent" with respect to pursuit of the good life.

Though wealth does not preclude the simple life advocated by Stoicism, ill-gotten gain and material sustenance via compromised values are certainly corrosive to virtue and contrary to the embodiment of correct moral purpose. Money has its admirable uses, but all too often, we are tempted to sacrifice our decency or allow a contamination of our character in order to obtain wealth that does not contribute to a life well lived. Stoic simplicity is, among other things, a refusal to accept complication and compromise in exchange for material gain. Socrates, a Stoic hero and moral exemplar, argues at his trial that most of his fellow Athenians irrationally value wealth, fame, and power more highly than virtue and wisdom – adding to their own decadence, as well as accelerating the decline of Athenian culture. From this error, all sorts of misfortune and misbehavior ensue, and Socrates seeks to awaken his fellow citizens to this inveterate and irrational tendency:

> I shall go on saying, in my usual way, My very good friend, you are an Athenian and belong to a city which is the greatest and most famous in the world for its wisdom and strength. Are you not ashamed that you give your attention to acquiring as much money as possible, and similarly with reputation and honor, and give no attention or thought to truth and understanding and the perfection of your soul?
>
> And if any of you disputes this and professes to care about these things, I shall not at once let him go or leave him. No, I shall question him and examine him and test him; and if it appears that in spite of his profession he has made no real progress toward goodness, I shall reprove him for neglecting what is of supreme importance, and giving his attention to trivialities. [*Apology*, 29d–30a, pp. 15–16]

Not even the threat of execution can dissuade Socrates from the dogged pursuit of wisdom and virtue. He knows that the jury and the hemlock cannot harm that which is inseparable from and constitutive of what Socrates refers to as his "soul." No one can force indecency, cowardice, or any other vice upon a virtuous man. The only person that one has the power to diminish, degrade, or devalue, is oneself. One's character is, therefore, the only proper object of one's most devout efforts to progress toward "perfection." In this respect, each of us is master of himself – provided that he takes the trouble and makes the effort necessary to develop robust mental discipline.

Stoic Freedom and Interpersonal Affairs

The Stoic's simple life cannot be realized without liberation from those constraints and complications that tend to generate needless stress and discontent, or to invite degradation. The desire for admiration, fame, or social status almost unavoidably entails compromise intended to please those upon whom such matters are dependent. Epictetus warns that this is a form of enslavement to values that may be incompatible with the pursuit of wisdom and virtue. In *A Guide to the Good Life: The Ancient Art of Stoic Joy*, William Irvine (2009) succinctly articulates this element of Stoic counsel:

> Stoics value their freedom, and they are therefore reluctant to do anything that will give others power over them. But if we seek social status, we give people power over us: We have to do things calculated to make them admire us, and we have to refrain from doing things that will trigger their disfavor. Epictetus therefore advises us not to seek social status, since if we make it our goal to please others, we will no longer be free to please ourselves. We will, he says, have enslaved ourselves. [2009, p. 167]

There is hardly a more pervasive instigation of needless complexity regarding the human condition than the urge to please other people (not to mention the psychological and emotional consequences of failures to satisfy that urge). No one can legitimately claim to be free while relinquishing his contentment to the passing interests and fickle tastes of those he hopes to impress. One cannot live simply and also seek the approval of persons who are obsessed with money, possessions, fame, power, status, and the other familiar objects of perennial worldly obsession – all of which necessitate some degree of guile, calculation, or pretense. It is also impossible to "be oneself," provided that one embraces Stoic values, while aiming to appeal to those who reject those values and embrace the general aspirations of the acquisitive and compulsively envious masses. We must begin to weave Shakespeare's tangled web of deception when we set out to win acclaim by concealing unpopular interests, such as the attainment of virtue, wisdom, and self-discipline, or when we feign interest in common desiderata such as wealth, fame, power, and social status.

Just as there is no incompatibility between Stoic simplicity and material wealth or power, similarly there is no necessary tension between Stoic simplicity and virtuous engagement in interpersonal relations or active participation in socio-political affairs (should one choose this course of endeavor). Marcus Aurelius was, after all, simultaneously a devoted Stoic practitioner, a husband, a father, and Emperor of the greatest socioeconomic and military power on the planet at the time. The philosopher king's simplicity is exhibited in his recognition that most of the world's affairs are beyond the control even of Rome's throne. He understood clearly that his position afforded him no power to determine anything beyond his own will, attitudes, desires, and other mental states. Even Caesar faces illness, aging, disloyalty, frustration, and death. Even Caesar is subject to nature and the winds and vicissitudes of fate. He knew himself to be no more than a man and, in the final analysis, no more capable of controlling external states of affairs than anyone else (appearances to the contrary notwithstanding). Commands may be disobeyed or misunderstood, legions may fail, and treachery may reach into the very pinnacle of power (the Emperor was well aware that more than one of his predecessors had met an untimely end at the hands of a trusted retinue). He understood the business of a man (any man) to be relatively simple (though not at all easy) and straightforward. In his *Meditations*, he reminds himself:

A man should habituate himself to such a way of thinking that if suddenly asked, "What is in your mind at this minute?" he could respond frankly and without hesitation; thus proving that all thoughts were simple and kindly... He does not forget the brotherhood of all rational beings, nor that a concern for every man is proper to humanity; and he knows that it is not the world's opinions he should follow... and the approval of such men, who do not even stand well in their own eyes, has no value for him. [Epictetus, 1944, 4]

Even if he lives in a palace, a man's sphere of direct influence extends no further than the reach of his will and assumes only those dimensions to which rigorous training may expand the perimeter of self-discipline:

Letting go all else, cling to the following few truths. Remember that man lives only in the present, in this fleeting instant: all the rest of his life is either past and gone, or not yet revealed. This mortal life is a little thing, lived in a little corner of the earth; and little, too, is the longest fame to come – dependent as it is on a succession of fast-perishing little men who have no knowledge even of their own selves, much less of one long dead and gone. [Epictetus, 1944, 10]

How many rulers of men display the capacity to recognize and embrace their own insignificance in the great and flowing course of events? The most influential man in the world calls his life "a little thing," conceives the Roman Empire as but "a little corner of the earth," and disdains fame as reliant upon the interests of "fast-perishing little men" – little men no different, ultimately, from himself. We see that a kind of modesty and contempt for self-aggrandizement is part of the Stoic conception of simplicity. Marcus Aurelius understands that he is no more significant than any other man, and claims no special standing merely because the fates have seen fit to place him in a position of terrestrial authority. One suspects that he would have written the same words had he been a shepherd, slave, merchant, or mid-level government functionary. Epictetus knew the slave's life from the first person perspective, but expressed much the same attitude regarding the fundamentals of the human condition, as did the Stoic who became Emperor. Such distinctions are simply irrelevant to one's proper conduct as a man and as a Stoic practitioner. Life is simplified by a consistent and devout focus upon those "few truths" of which the simple, wise man (be he slave or Emperor) assiduously reminds himself.

Conclusion

The Roman Stoics valued virtue and sought freedom from all-too-common vices, such as pretense, greed, and indiscipline. The often-underappreciated virtue of simplicity is central to the Stoic conception of the well-lived life. A simple life is devoid of needless and unhealthy obsession with elements of the external world that lie beyond the agent's control. In particular, embracing simplicity entails a rationally governed indifference to social status as well as to the opinions and attitudes of others, thus providing liberation from common anxieties and ignoble efforts to attain fame, fortune, or material advantage. The Emperor, Marcus Aurelius, admired the former slave, Epictetus, and, in his *Meditations*, expressed gratitude for the latter's wise counsel. Both were simple men, but the attainment and perfection of Stoic simplicity was (and remains) no simple matter.

Stoic "Harm" as Degradation

It is crucial to note that Epictetus advises the Stoic practitioner to restrict his desires and aversions to "internals" (i.e. conditions that are directly subject to, and determined by, the agent's will), and to cultivate *rational* intentions that "accord with nature" or the Logos as it is manifest in persons. Thus, the Stoic must direct his mental energy and exert intense effort regarding the development of mental discipline and self-rectification. Epictetus does *not* instruct his students to simply accept any and all conditions as they arise, but his injunction to "wish for events to happen as they do happen" amounts to cultivating rational indifference regarding *externals* (i.e. conditions that are *not* subject to the agent's will) while focusing a disciplined will on maintaining imperturbability and integrity irrespective of conditions over which one simply has no control.

This injunction generalizes to *all* external conditions, including potential permutations of nuclear strike and/or terrorist attack scenarios, any Zombie Apocalypse one might imagine, the reanimation and public befouling of one's corpse, and even (the Fates preserve us) Paris Hilton's unseemly exploits. All such conditions are outside the sphere of the agent's direct control and are, therefore, not proper objects of the Stoic's concern. A world populated by flesh-eating Zombies may result in physical damage to one's corporeal self (not to mention severe limitations upon one's viable vacation options), but this does not constitute *harm* according to the Stoic (not to mention Socratic) understanding of the *true* self. The concept often presented in English translations of Stoic texts as "harm" would, perhaps, be rendered more helpfully as "degradation" or "abasement." No external power can *degrade* a good Stoic who is self-possessed and living in accordance with Nature (Reason, the Logos) – just as Socrates insisted at his trial that a good man cannot be harmed by a bad man (though the good man *can*, Socrates noted, be killed, tortured, deprived of property, rights, etc.). The Stoic practitioner who develops sufficient self-mastery to properly govern his will with respect to phenomena regarding which the will has purchase cannot be *degraded* (i.e. truly *harmed*) by anyone. If a Stoic practitioner is degraded, it can only be by himself and some failure of his self-discipline or weakness of his own character. One may diminish or abase oneself through indiscipline, irrationality, and subsequent lapses in behavior and deportment. Other persons, however, can only alter *external* conditions, but can never reach into the "inner citadel" of the competent Stoic's well-trained character. Epictetus was born into slavery, but the conditions of his birth could not degrade or diminish his character, his decency, or his will (the crucial objects of Stoic concern), and only his body could be bound in chains or broken by torture. No man ever enslaved his *true* self – his indomitable will. Epictetus, like Socrates before him, feared no condition of the external world or assault upon body, reputation, or property. These are trifling ephemera "on loan" (but briefly) from Nature. One has the power (or can develop the mental discipline necessary to exercise the power) to govern only those conditions that are directly determined by one's will, thus only such phenomena are truly "one's own." It follows then that one can be harmed only insofar as one degrades oneself through the irrational misdirection of one's will and the failure of proper self-governance. A true sage, therefore, suffers no harm and lives free of fear and perturbation. The external world will have its way with matters beyond one's sphere of control (e.g. body, reputation, environment), but the Stoic sage does not contend against the world or external events as Nature (or Zeus, or the Logos) dictates that they shall be. The devout and dedicated Stoic practitioner seeks to be master of himself (i.e. to cultivate a rationally directed will) – and mortal man can aspire to no greater achievement than that.

Free Will, Determinism, and Stoic Counsel

But our souls are... joined to God, as being indeed members and distinct portions of his essence.
– Epictetus [*Discourses*, Book I, 14]

Determinism often meets the charge that, if true, it would render all purposive deliberation and effort futile. If all that occurs is necessitated by laws of nature, antecedent conditions, the will of God, the gods, Fate, or any other form of cosmic governance, then it seems that the course of one's life, as it is but a tiny stream of events in confluence with all other streams in the deterministic universe, must *a fortiori* be fixed by whatever forces guide the course and flow of *all* events. So, if all events in the universe are determined, and one's life is a series of events within the universe, then one's life will unfold as necessitated by the irresistible powers that be, and attempts to master one's own fate are futile or even perverse. As determinists, the ancient Stoics were familiar with this complaint, and Susanne Bobzien notes that Origen, in *Against Celsus*, mentions the following "Idle Argument" as an alleged sophism with which determinists were frequently confronted:

(1) If it is fated that you will recover from this illness, then, regardless of whether you consult a doctor or you do not consult <a doctor> you will recover.

(2) But also: if it is fated that you won't recover from this illness, then, regardless of whether you consult a doctor or you do not consult <a doctor> you won't recover.

(3) But either it is fated that you will recover from this illness or it is fated that you will not recover <from this illness>.

(4) Therefore it is futile to consult a doctor. [1998, p. 182]

5

The objection is, of course, intended to generalize to all decisions, deliberations, efforts and exertions. Bobzien again nicely draws out this generalized intent of the indeterminist stratagem:

> The ancients seem usually not to have bothered with universalization or with extracting a scheme, but to have standardly used a paradigmatic argument as representative for a class of arguments. It becomes clear from Cicero *Fat.* 30 that the Idle Argument was understood in this way. There Cicero talks of different cases of a genus of sophism of which the presented argument is one... Still, we can extract a general scheme, and the following one may do:
>
> (P1) If it is fated that A, then, whether or not you Φ, A.
> (P2) If it is fated that not-A, then, whether or not you Φ, not A.
> (P3) Either it is fated that A or it is fated that not-A.
> (P4) Therefore (with regard to A) it is futile (for you) to Φ.
> [pp. 183–4]

So, Stoic philosophy was charged with an incompatibility between its deterministic worldview and its advocacy of various methods of self-discipline aiming at self-improvement:

> In their ethical theory the Stoics demand that people perform certain actions in a certain way in order to realize certain objectives... and thereby to strive at reaching a certain end (e.g. conformity with Nature). The same action would thus be described as both futile and morally commanded or commended. [p. 191]

So, one may be commanded to do that which cannot be done or that which can be done, but only futilely so, as its aim is contrary to Fate or the will of Zeus.

Determinism and Stoic Counsel

In the opening entry of the *Enchiridion*, we find Epictetus admonishing his students to be careful to distinguish between those things that are within their power and those things that are not:

> Now, the things within our power are by nature free, unrestricted, unhindered; but those beyond our power are weak, dependent, restricted, alien. Remember, then, that if you attribute freedom to things by nature dependent, and take what belongs to others for your own, you will be hindered, you will lament, you will be disturbed, you will find fault both with gods and men. But if you take for your own only that which is your own, and view what belongs to others just as it really is, then no one will ever compel you, no one will restrict you, you will find fault with no one, you will accuse no one, you will do nothing against your will; no one will hurt you, you will not have an enemy, nor will you suffer any harm. [*Enchiridion*, 1]

So, the wise never fail to see their desires satisfied and never experience anything to which they are averse, because the wise only desire goods that lie within their power and are only averse to evils which are within their power to avoid. Students are then advised to concern themselves only with that which is "up to them," or within their power, and to remain blissfully indifferent to all "externals." The only rational concern for the wise man is that which is subject to his will and controlled by its dictates. It is foolish, wasteful, and unhealthy to trouble oneself over events that lie beyond one's sphere of direct control. So, Epictetus advises his philosophers in training.

At the end of the *Enchiridion*, however, we find Epictetus advising his students to keep at the ready maxims such as this one from the "Hymn of Cleanthes":

Conduct me, Zeus, and thou, O Destiny,
Wherever *your decrees have fixed my lot.*
I follow cheerfully; and, did I not,
Wicked and wretched, I must follow still. [*Enchiridion*, 52 – emphasis added]

This maxim extends Chrysippus' contention, as related in Cicero's *On Fate*, that "whatever happens, happens by fate." Similarly, the oft-quoted remark about the dog and the cart, generally attributed to either Zeno or Chrysippus, asserts the same thoroughgoing determinism (if not fatalism). Marcus Aurelius in his *Meditations* insists that:

Providence is the source from which all things flow; and allied with it is Necessity, and the welfare of the universe. You yourself are a part of that universe; and for any one of nature's parts, that which is assigned to it by the World-Nature or helps to keep it in being is good. [Book Two, 3]

Zeus, World-Nature, Fate, the *Logos* – by any name, the intelligence or force directing the universe – determines the unfolding and pattern of all events. The sage recognizes this and achieves peace and equanimity by "yielding to Fate" and embracing the world as it is. But, of course, the sage is part of the world and embedded within its guided evolution. So, the *Handbook* opens with a bit of advice that appears to conflict with its closing, apparently fatalistic, maxims. We are advised to focus on that which we can directly control, but are also reminded that all events are fixed by Fate. The sphere of one's direct control would, therefore, seem to contract to the vanishing point.

If the unfolding evolution of the entire universe and, *ipso facto*, the course of each individual's life within the universe is ultimately determined by forces that lie beyond the individual's control, then it is, at best, pointless (and, at worst incoherent and/

or perverse) to recommend any particular course of behavior or method of self-discipline – as each of us is fated to be as Fate (or Zeus) will have him be. It is, moreover, self-contradictory to hold persons responsible for adhering to counsel regarding their behavior and attitude if forces beyond their control ultimately determine that their behavior and attitude will not conform to counsel. One does not, after all, counsel a river in hopes of changing its course.

Many of Stoicism's detractors (as well as those who object to any form of determinism), past and present, have fastened on this putative inconsistency and presented it as an insoluble difficulty for the Stoic worldview. Stoicism, these critics claim, must either give up the doctrine of causal determinism or, in retaining determinism, must admit that its counsels regarding self-rectification are impotent (as impotence is commonly implicated in failures of rectification). So goes the complaint.

It has often been (and still often is) assumed that attempts at self-improvement presuppose and require the existence of a free will, an "open" future, and choices unconstrained (or, at least, uncompelled) by antecedent conditions and natural law (or God's laws as embodied in natural regularities). It is sometimes assumed, that is, that counsel and training are pointless without free will. This assumption invites scrutiny.

Why must the Stoic embrace the existence of free will in order to consistently offer or employ counsel concerning the conduct and course of a good life in accordance with reason and nature? While many Stoic philosophers apparently attempted to carve out some sphere of freedom of the will that could coexist with an otherwise universal determinism, I argue that nothing about Stoic counsel and its supposed efficacy for producing equanimity and happiness requires the existence of free will or a rejection of universal determinism. In short, I argue that the Stoics should have (or at least *could* have) rejected freedom of the will while defending Stoicism's efficacy for producing a well-ordered mind, virtuous character, and a life of harmony with Nature.

Rectification and Freedom

It is important to note that the purported benefits of Stoic counsel are putatively derived from a proper alignment of the agent's desires, expectations, and attitudes – but not necessarily from a freely and "openly" chosen alignment. The ideal Stoic sage has learned to distinguish between those things that are subject to his will and those things that are not. His desire and aversion attach only to that which is directly within his control, and all else is embraced as in conformity with the perfect rational direction of the *Logos* (or the regularities of Nature as the manifestation of Zeus' will). The sage controls what he can and remains serenely detached from all that does not directly conform to his will. He is thereby liberated from psychological and emotional distress. This liberation does not require freedom of the will or the absence of determinants antecedent to any act of will. Stoic counsel's efficacy requires only that attitudes, desires, and aversions may be altered by the power of argument, reason, and techniques of behavioral conditioning. If the student's attitudes, and behavior can be modified by dint of dialogue, study, practice, etc., then Stoic counsel can improve that student's self-control, mental rectitude, and ultimately the student's overall well-being. These alterations to character, behavioral dispositions, desires, and aversions need not be voluntarily or freely adopted in order that they effect positive change. If, for example, a modern Stoic neurosurgeon could render his patient perfectly rational by virtue of a comprehensive surgical "rewiring" of the brain and its connections to the sensory periphery, then a sage (or, at least, a functional equivalent thereof) would emerge from a process that no one would be inclined to regard as issuing from that new sage's *free* will. His sagacity would be causally determined by the neurosurgery that produced it. He would not, for that reason, be any less wise, rational, or healthy.

The relevant adjustments in the patient's beliefs and attitudes can, according to Stoic philosophers, eventuate without opening the skull and slicing into the brain, by virtue of training in logical analysis and the application thereof to the fundamental nature of the external world and of its relationship to the self. In his *Discourses*, Epictetus points out that this training is intended to improve the student's capacity for self-rectification:

> It is not understood by most persons that the proper use of arguments by inference and hypothesis and interrogations, and logical forms generally, has any relation to the duties of life. In every matter the question is, how a wise and good man may go honestly and consistently through with it. [Book I, 7]

It is the proper *alignment* of the will and the intellect that liberates the agent from needless suffering and enables him to live "honestly and consistently." Whether this alignment is attained freely or via external compulsion is simply beside the point – just as a patient need not consent in order that the surgeon's scalpel extract a tumor or rectify an impediment to blood flow. Similarly, free consent is not a necessary condition for the extirpation of unhealthy mental tendencies.

The Stoic's art is really the art of instruction, training, and discipline. The sage effectively disciplines his mind and conditions his will so as to respond to the vicissitudes of daily life with reason and equanimity. The Stoic teacher instructs the student in the theory, practice, and methodology of this form of rational self-control. Neither the instructor nor the student needs to possess a free will in order to produce the desired outcome. The will need not be free in order for it to be brought into concordance with Nature or with the *Logos*, or the will of Zeus. There is nothing incoherent about a sage who is determined to develop self-control *through the exertion of mental effort*. His reason is the proximal director of his behavior and his will, though Zeus is the ultimate, distal director of all events – including those constituting the creation and evolution of the sage. Keith Seddon points out the intimate relation in Stoic theology between the will of Zeus and the guiding reason within each person:

> The Stoics identified *logos* (reason), fate and god, regarding them as different aspects of the one principle which creates and sustains the world... God, through acting on passive unqualified substance, makes it what it is. But since god is considered to be a *body*, and is co-extensive with the world and is "in" everything, god must also be in *us*. The Stoics believed that the governing part of each human soul, the *hegemonikon*, is a fragment of the divine *logos*. [2004, p. 7]

So, the individual human's *hegemonikon* directs his behavior, attitudes, etc., but only wisely and healthily so insofar as his "governing part" is in harmony with the will of the all-directing God. It is God's will that individual persons shall govern themselves. Each "governing part" is a fragment of the *divine* governance.

An analogy with animal training may be instructive here. A dog's master can, for example, condition his pet to "do its business" outside – and not on the shag carpet in the living room. Various methods might successfully effect this change in the dog's behavior, and none of them require that the dog freely adopt a change of heart regarding the sanctity of shag carpet or the propriety of relieving itself outdoors. External pressures are applied in the form of punishments and/or rewards until the dog's natural inclinations have been brought into conformity with her master's desires. The dog's behavior is "rectified" through an external imposition of conditions that generate an internal alteration of inclinations and proclivities – and, *voila*, good dog! Nor is it necessary that the dog's master freely engage in the project of training the pet. A master that has been given a post-hypnotic instruction and manipulated by the hypnotist can, in principle, effect the same change in the dog's behavior as can any other master. The hypnotist may, in turn, be subject to deterministic control by another external force, with further iterations *ad infinitum*. Nowhere would such a chain of decisions and modifications of behavior be "open," uncompelled, or "free" in any robust sense – yet dog and master are both better off.

Determinism and Self-Control

Determinists do not, after all, hold that a particular event is determined to occur irrespective of antecedents, but rather that a particular event occurs precisely because of the complex interplay between a chain (or web) of antecedents, consequents, and the laws, principles, or other mechanisms governing the interrelations among them. The Stoics do not claim that the will of Zeus is brought to fruition through scattershot, isolated moments of divine intervention in an otherwise chaotic universe. The Stoic God is not a cosmic pointillist leaving suggestive gaps of indeterminacy between occasional ordered atoms of time and space. The world, according to the Stoics, unfolds as a smooth, harmonious confluence of perfectly ordered streams of events. *All* events are directed by the will of Zeus, and are fated to occur because their antecedents and concomitants appear precisely as they do. The instructor encounters the student at the time and place of Zeus' choosing. The student is thereby improved, or not, as necessitated by the divine, all-encompassing master plan – a plan that includes the exertion of effort by various performers in the production.

Every event in any agent's life is an antecedent condition for all subsequent events. If antecedent conditions and laws of nature, as ordained by Zeus, determine the course of all events, then encounters with Stoic counsel are part of the complex web of causal antecedents determining the student's future behavior, mental states, interaction with environmental stimuli, etc. Advice, instruction, and other techniques of conditioning all have some role to play in the unfolding of the Master's grand production – in which each of us is but a player assigned some role of the Designer's choosing. The buffoon's beliefs, attitudes, desires, and aversions may be altered, if Zeus decrees that it be so, *by* his encounters with the wise and their instruction, and *by* his efforts thereafter. Stoic counsel plays the educational role that it does because Zeus requires teachers and students to appear as they do, and when they do, so that His overarching design may come to fruition. The efforts of the learned and the still learning, far from being futile, idle, or pointless, are requisite elements of the grand design. The will of Zeus flows through all of his creation, and each evolving human character is carried along in its current. The sage does not need a *free* will, but only a will directed by right reason in accordance with God's nature. A sage may be born and, more often, a sage may be made, but a sage is a sage nonetheless, and God makes it so through His will as manifest in His guided creation – of which we are part and in which we all live.

God or Atoms: Stoic Counsel With or Without Zeus

Recall to thy recollection this alternative; either there is providence or atoms, fortuitous concurrence of things; or remember the arguments by which it has been proved that the world is a kind of political community, and be quiet at last.
– Marcus Aurelius [*Meditations* 4:3]

There is wide agreement that ethics is independent of religion. (And we [modern Stoics] certainly concur.)
– Lawrence Becker [1998, p. 8]

"Following nature", or "following the gods", in the Stoic sense, amounts to... serene acceptance of things that lie outside of our direct control.
– Donald Robertson [2010, p. 11]

Most ancient Stoics believed in a God of some description or other (mostly pantheistic in nature), and most conceived of Stoic practical counsel within the framework of a rationally ordered and governed cosmos. A properly managed human life must "accord with Nature" or with "the Logos" or with "the will of Zeus" as the rational ordering principle underpinning an intentionally and felicitously structured cosmos. We must, the Stoics counselled, understand humanity's role within the natural order, and conduct ourselves according to Nature's dictates as reasoning beings in pursuit of virtue or excellence. The ancient Stoics believed that they lived in God's world – or a world that existed as a physical manifestation of the divine. Does it follow, then, that the efficacy of Stoic counsel is inextricably dependent upon some form of intelligent design or teleological cosmology? Is Stoic counsel groundless and inefficacious without God (or

47

Zeus) and the pervasive Logos governing the unfolding of events? I will argue that it is not. Indeed, I will make the case that metaphysical doctrines about the nature and existence of God, and a rationally governed cosmos, are rather cleanly separable from Stoic practical counsel, and its conductivity to a well-lived, *eudaimonistic* life. Several ancient Stoic philosophers suggested that Stoic practical counsel remains efficacious in the absence of a Creator or Designer. As Donald Robertson points out in *The Philosophy of Cognitive-Behavioural Therapy (CBT)*:

> Certain Stoics appear to have been willing to contemplate agnosticism or atheism as consistent with their philosophy. As Marcus Aurelius repeats to himself, whether the universe is "God or atoms," either way the basic precepts of Stoicism still stand firm. [2010, p. 56]

Robertson further indicates that Zeno, the putative founder of Stoicism, is alleged to have declared that the divinity of nature (or the author thereof) is inessential to Stoic counsel:

> The references to "God" in Stoicism, to put it bluntly, could probably be replaced by the word "Nature" or "the Universe" without much loss of meaning, as Zeno himself says, and doing so would probably render things much easier to digest for modern CBT practitioners. [p. 56]

So too, I argue, for contemporary Stoics – and for much the same reason. A sage is no less sagacious in the absence of God, Zeus, Providence, or teleological cosmology. Progress toward the regulative ideal of the Stoic sage is marked and measured in a manner not dissimilar from the measurements of progress in modern CBT. Stoicism may have developed within a worldview infused with presuppositions of a divinely-ordered universe, and, indeed, there *may* be a Creator or Designer of some type (I take no position, in this paper, regarding the existence of God), but the efficacy of Stoic counsel is not *dependent* upon creation, design, or any form of intelligent cosmological guidance. The Stoic practitioner does not require a divine stamp of approval to legitimize his pursuit of equanimity, excellence, and wise self-governance.

Agnostic *Eudaimonism*

There either is or is not a God, a Creator or Designer of the Cosmos, and an arbiter and judge of propriety in the conduct of human affairs. Insofar as the practical applications of Stoicism to the ubiquitous challenges of the human condition are concerned, however, the existence or nonexistence of God is less than paramount. Indeed, as the aforementioned epigraph from Marcus Aurelius suggests, propriety in our day-to-day conduct, and the maintenance of reason, resolve, and dignity, are not obviously contingent upon the transcendent or the pervasive presence of the divine at all. My contention is that virtue (for lack of a better term) is conceived within Stoicism as its own reward, irrespective of possibilities regarding external reward or punishment, and it is to be cultivated assiduously and in earnest regardless of anyone else's judgment. Should our virtue please God (or Zeus, or conform to the Logos) as well, then so much the better (or, at least, none the worse). Should there be no God to judge us, we still have, according to Stoicism, every bit as much reason and motivation to improve our character, to develop self-mastery, to increase in virtue, and to conduct ourselves with dignity and integrity as best we are able. Contemporary practitioners of Stoicism, or those simply seeking to incorporate Stoic practice, and Stoic insight into the conduct and management of their daily lives, need not hesitate due to skepticism regarding the existence of a Creator (or Designer) of the universe. The presence or absence of a divine Judge of human conduct is external to the will and control of the Stoic agent. Indeed, those who wish to selectively adopt only certain elements of the Stoic worldview, and cherry-pick elements of Stoic practice, rather than adopt Stoicism *tout court*, are also free to do so (indeed, I hope to *encourage* them to do so) irrespective of belief in, or rejection of, any divine, transcendent, or otherwise celestially coordinating intelligence. My thesis is not intended to suggest that belief in God is irrational or indefensible, but merely to make the case that such belief is not *necessary* for rigorous and efficacious Stoic practice. Lawrence Becker touches on the increasingly secularized worldview of his audience in his recent work, *A New Stoicism*:

> There is a complex and interesting debate, among scholars of the ancient stoic texts, about whether stoic ethics is eudaimonistic through and through, or whether the stoic conception of the cosmos as a rational and purposive entity makes it difficult to assimilate stoicism straightforwardly to (other) ancient eudaimonistic theories... The issue is nearly moot here, however, since we now reject the early cosmic teleology, and since all hands agree that stoic ethical theory grows out of what we now identify as the eudaimonistic tradition, and gives a developmental account of virtue... that is thoroughly eudaimonistic. [1998, pp. 25–26]

Eudaimonia, or (roughly) a well-lived, flourishing life, is described primarily, if not entirely, in terms of developing and enacting virtuous character, and it is stipulated that virtue is not dependent upon, and is separable from, the pantheistic conception of God or a rationally governed cosmos. So, a synoptic Stoic ethic, and the practice entailed thereby, need not atrophy before a cultural milieu that seems increasingly detached from concerns involving the divine or transcendent realm. Stoic ethics is clearly compatible with the existence of a pantheistic God (indeed most ancient Stoics appear to have subscribed to some version of pantheism), but belief in God is neither necessary as a prerequisite, nor required as a correlate of the Stoic conception of virtue, and no specific metaphysical commitment is a necessary precondition to the efficacy of Stoic practical counsel.

Roman Stoicism Among the Atoms

There are intimations of the detachability of Stoic counsel from metaphysical commitments in the writings of the later Roman Stoics. Well aware of the Epicurean suggestion that the universe is an unguided ensemble of atoms, and a realm into which the gods (if they exist) do not deign to encroach, Marcus Aurelius considered the possibility of a natural world, absent creation or design, and concluded that Stoic practice would serve just as well with or without God in the picture.

> If a thing is in thy own power, why dost thou do it? But if it is in the power of another, whom dost thou blame? The atoms (chance) or the gods? Both are foolish. Thou must blame nobody. For if thou canst, correct that which is the cause; but if thou canst not do this, correct at least the thing itself; but if thou canst not do even this, of what use is it to thee to find fault? For nothing should be done without a purpose. [*Meditations*, 8:17]

Though Marcus himself appears fairly confident that God orders and ordains events in the world in which we find ourselves embedded, he clearly does not regard intelligent design and guidance as a sine qua non of Stoic principles of propriety in matters of self-governance. It is, of course, self-rectification and the development of virtue or excellence that reside at the very heart of Stoic counsel. Thus, the first bit of guidance offered in Epictetus' *Enchiridion* is:

> Now, the things within our power are by nature free,

unrestricted, unhindered; but those beyond our power are weak, dependent, restricted, alien. Remember, then, that if you attribute freedom to things by nature dependent, and take what belongs to others for your own, you will be hindered, you will lament, you will be disturbed, you will find fault both with gods and men. But if you take for your own only that which is your own, and view what belongs to others just as it really is, then no one will ever compel you, no one will restrict you, you will find fault with no one, you will accuse no one, you will do nothing against your will; no one will hurt you, you will not have an enemy, nor will you suffer any harm. [*Enchiridion*, 1]

Physics and logic have their role in Stoic theory, but that role, especially in later Roman Stoicism, is always conceived as subordinate to the purpose of practical counsel regarding the Stoic's conduct and mental discipline. A grasp of issues that we would, today, regard as matters of metaphysics and epistemology serve the ultimate goal of self-rectification, and progress toward the (perhaps unattainable) aim of becoming a Stoic sage. Even if true, unblemished sagacity is attainable by very few or, indeed, none, setting this condition as a regulatory ideal encourages sincere, sustained effort – without which, progress is likely to be stultified or anemic. Socrates, Heraclitus, Diogenes, Epictetus, and Cato the Younger may (or may not) have embraced the conception of a rationally governed universe, but these exemplars of the Stoic ideal were revered for their conduct, lionized for their courage, and admired for their self-discipline and independence of thought. The lives they lived either stand or fall as legitimate examples of moral rectitude whether the gods in which they (may have) believed are actual, or were mere projections of the collective cultural imaginations of their respective societies. Heroic character does not dissolve in naturalism, or corrode with exposure to contemporary developments in our understanding of the human condition. Our current understanding of the nature of the world in which we find ourselves embedded is tangential to a proper consideration and assessment of any individual's character.

Eudaimonism is concerned, first and foremost, with the attainment of well-being or, at the very least, conducting oneself in a manner that approximates, as closely as possible, a flourishing human life. If a human assemblage of atoms, endowed with sentience and reason, can attain better or worse states of being, and if wisdom and virtue can be exemplified irrespective of any cosmological "design plan," then Stoic *eudaimonia* is no less comprehensible than Epicurean or Aristotelian conceptions of well-being, or the respective practices of the Epicurean and Peripatetic philosophers. If Epictetus is a near approximation of a Stoic sage, then his stature and his virtue are not diminished by states of affairs beyond his control. Such external conditions include the presence or absence of a divine Orderer of the cosmos.

Epictetus often describes the benefits of Stoic practice in terms that make no reference to anything beyond the terrestrial realm and augmentation of the practitioner's well-being:

> So, in our own case, we take it to be the work of one who studies philosophy to bring his will into harmony with events; so that none of the things which happen may happen against our inclination, nor those which do not happen be desired by us. Hence they who have settled this point have it in their power never to be disappointed in what they seek, nor to incur what they shun; but to lead their own lives without sorrow, fear, or perturbation, and in society to preserve all the natural or acquired relations of son, father, brother, citizen, husband, wife, neighbor, fellow traveler, ruler, or subject. Something like this is what we take to be the work of a philosopher. [*Discourses*, p. 122]

Thus, the promise of Stoic practice is presented in pragmatic terms. The goal is self-improvement, freedom from "perturbation," and virtue in all "natural or acquired relations." The Stoic seeks to become a *better person* – irrespective of external judgment.

Contemporary Stoicism

The modern Stoic may subscribe to a religious worldview such as Judaism, Christianity, Islam, Hinduism, or Buddhism. There is little in the fundamental tenets of these wisdom traditions that does not comport fairly readily with the project of Stoic self-mastery. Indeed, several historical figures seem to have been enamored of both Stoicism and one of the major world religions. Examples include (arguably) Philo of Alexandria, Justus Lipsius, Michel de Montaigne, and Mohandas Gandhi. The degree to which some of these figures embraced and enacted a Stoic ethic is disputable, but such disputes are less than central to the current inquiry. More to my primary point regarding contemporary Stoicism is the separability of Stoic ethics and, particularly, Stoic self-rectification, from a religious worldview or any specific attendant metaphysical commitments. Modern persons need not curtail their curiosity about Stoic cognitive and behavioral exercises due to frequent mentions of Zeus or the Logos found in Epictetus, Marcus Aurelius, or Seneca. It would be, in my judgment, something of a shame if those seeking wise, efficacious counsel about the human condition, its all-too-common infirmities, and the attainment of equanimity despite relentless challenges, turned away from Stoic counsel due to the misconception that Stoic practice necessitates an acceptance of religious commitments that many contemporary minds find quaint, archaic, or anathema. In other words, budding Stoics should not be forestalled in their development simply because they do not believe in Zeus (or *any* God). One need not embrace Biblical literalism to benefit from observing the Ten Commandments, and one need not believe in the Greek gods to emulate Epictetus' resilience, reason, and resolve. It is possible to be a "Modern Marcus" without subscribing to the belief that one is endowed with a "spark of the divine." A contemporary Seneca need not regard reason as a gift from the Creator, in order to exercise reason in the conduct of a dignified life, or in the maintenance of virtuous character. In short, Stoic counsel has "no need of that hypothesis" for which Laplace famously could identify no necessary explanatory role in his cosmology. We Twenty-First Century Stoics need not blush at the mention of ancient theories concerning divine teleology, any more than Twenty-First Century physicists need blush at the mention of Newton's apparent interest in alchemy. Stoic counsel is exportable from the Graeco-Roman cultural milieu, and it is readily portable as well. We can take it with us from place to place, sustain our serenity with it through trying times, and use it to improve our forbearance with those who ridicule Stoicism as an outmoded relic of ancient, benighted "counselors of the soul" (whether we believe in literal souls or not). John Sellars identifies the maintenance of rational self-governance as the centerpiece of Roman Stoic counsel:

> Thus, for that rational being – i.e. the philosopher – only this excellence (ἀρετή) is judged to be good. Those objects of one's primary impulses such as food or health or wealth, although apparently beneficial to every human being, do not contribute to the preservation of a rational being *qua* rational being. They only contribute to its survival *qua* animal.
>
> This theory forms the basis for the famous Stoic claim that only virtue or excellence (ἀρετή) is good and that all other apparently beneficial entities are strictly speaking indifferent. Although the philosopher may prefer to be healthy and wealthy than not – hence their status as "preferred indifferents" – these things are not strictly speaking good because they do not contribute to the preservation of his own

constitution insofar as he is a rational being. [2009, p. 58]

If health and wealth cannot be more than "preferred indifferents," as they lie outside of the agent's direct sphere of control and depend upon conditions not subject to determination by the agent's will, and if all such phenomena "do not contribute to the preservation of his own constitution insofar as he is a rational being," then it would appear to follow that the condition of adherence to "the will of Zeus" must also fall, at best, into the category of "preferred indifferents." The existence or nonexistence of Zeus, or *any* God, is not subject to the agent's will. Thus, an action or mental posture's compliance with the dictates of Zeus, or *any* external entity, is *a fortiori* not subject to the agent's will, and cannot "contribute to the preservation of a rational being *qua* rational being." It follows that "pleasing Zeus" cannot be "strictly speaking *good*," but must be relegated to the realm of the "preferred indifferent" (and *that*, only if Zeus exists). The *only* good is excellence (ἀρετή). The only proper Stoic goal is the improvement of one's character – irrespective of God's presence or absence from one's world.

Conclusion

Stoic counsel requires remarkably little "modernization" to address contemporary challenges of the human condition. This is not terribly surprising. For all of humanity's technological advancement throughout the millennia, we remain relatively small, physically fragile creatures embedded within a world that may or may not take heed of our existence or our struggles. How does one best live in this often cold, cruel (and, perhaps, unguided) world? One practices self-mastery and tries assiduously to increase one's rational excellence. One cultivates a virtuous character as best one can. If our world is nothing but a happenstance assemblage of atoms, so be it. One can live a better or worse life, a more or less skillful life, a more or less serene life, and a rational life, irrespective of the nature of ultimate reality. Whether the universe is a creation of God or a haphazard jumble of atoms, we find ourselves here, confronted with the world as it stands. Why should we not live according to reason? Whether the world and ourselves are designed by God, or are the result of unguided interactions of atoms and natural law, the rational human life holds out the hope of *eudaimonia*, flourishing, or living well. Any other life not rationally examined is, as Socrates insisted, "not worth living."

Stoic Counsel for Interpersonal Relations

There are things which are within our power, and there are things which are beyond our power.
– Epictetus

One of Epictetus' students, the historian Flavius Arrian, has selected this most fundamental fact of the human condition as the very first line of his teacher's *Enchiridion* or *Handbook* – a distillation of the main themes found in the former slave's lessons concerning Stoicism and the proper conduct of a rational life. With this staggeringly simple, but enormously potent and widely applicable bit of wisdom, the *Enchiridion*'s editor directs our focus to the first and most indispensable principle of Stoic counsel. Whatever the difficulty, whatever the circumstance, however one may have arrived at the current impasse or crisis, we are reminded that not everything is ours to control. Though nearly everyone will give verbal assent to this proposition, we seem inveterately to forget or to ignore its significance – and, in doing so, we subject ourselves repeatedly to needless emotional suffering and psychological trauma. When we lose sight of the fundamental limitations on our powers and the boundaries of our sphere of direct influence, feelings of frustration, anger, guilt, and hopelessness are almost certain to ensue. With a sustained awareness of our limitations and a clearheaded focus on those things that directly conform to the will, we can learn to dramatically ameliorate the psychological and emotional distress from which Stoic counsel promises relief.

Epictetus goes on to delineate a distinction between those phenomena that lie within the direct power of the human will, and those that lie beyond it:

Within our power are opinion, aim, desire, aversion, and, in one word, whatever affairs are our own. Beyond our power are body, property, reputation, office, and, in one word, whatever are not properly our own affairs. [*Enchiridion*, I]

The reference to "our own affairs" appears intended to pick out only those elements of the human condition that Epictetus believes to be entirely determined, without mediation, by exertion of the agent's will alone. Any feature of the world that is in any way dependent upon anything external to the agent's will is designated as "not properly our own affairs". The reader is then warned about the consequences of failing to appreciate the distinction:

Remember, then, that if you attribute freedom to things by nature dependent, and take what belongs to others for your own, you will be hindered, you will lament, you will be disturbed, you will find fault both with gods and men. But if you take for your own only that which is your own, and view what belongs to others just as it really is, then no one will ever compel you, no one will restrict you, you will find fault with no one, you will accuse no one, you will do nothing against your will; no one will hurt you, you will not have an enemy, nor will you suffer any harm. [*Enchiridion*, I]

In other words, Epictetus suggests that it is irrational, and detrimental to one's psychological and emotional well-being to trouble oneself with anything that does not directly answer to the exertion of one's will. The ideally rational man will control that which is entirely a matter of his own choosing, and will remain imperturbable by anything that he cannot directly control through the force of his will alone. Hence, the ideally rational man will not suffer psychological or emotional trauma. If a desirable state of affairs can be produced by a rational direction of his mind, the rational man will produce the desired state of affairs by exerting his will – and all else will be regarded with detached indifference. He will thereby achieve an unwavering equanimity irrespective of the vicissitudes of his interactions with the external world and, particularly as concerns the thesis of this paper, with the people he encounters therein.

Some, myself included, may remain skeptical of Epictetus' claim that opinion, desire, aversion and such are as entirely and ultimately within our power as he makes them out to be. Reconciling this sphere of individual control with the Stoic doctrine of causal determinism is notoriously problematic, and the issue has received ample treatment elsewhere.[1] Long before depth psychology and revelations from the cognitive sciences cast widespread doubt in the modern academic mind as to the freedom of the will and its independence from antecedent circumstances and environmental impingements, the ancient Stoics and their antagonists were aware of this potential difficulty for the Stoic worldview. Various debates arose among the competing Hellenistic schools concerning the apparent inconsistency between a universe bound by fate and the putative existence of freedom within the "inner citadel" of the mind. Can persons be free in any sense at all if they live in a deterministic universe? Fortunately, we are not required to defend any particular position regarding this matter in order to appreciate and implement Epictetus' negative injunction about attachments to matters beyond our control.

Though legitimate disputes exist concerning determinism, freedom of the will, and related issues, nearly everyone will agree that most events are beyond the direct control of any individual agent insofar as most of the universe clearly does not conform to any particular person's will. The central Stoic contention is that a little reflection should reveal that most of what we trouble ourselves about is quite clearly beyond our sphere of direct influence. As Epictetus points out, one's "body, property, reputation, office," and all other "externals" are subject to forces beyond one's control, and do not always obey one's will or coincide with one's desires. So all the energy spent in futile efforts to control phenomena and events that are not, in actuality, subject to one's control, and all psychological and emotional attachment to conditions obtaining in the external world (or failing to obtain therein) is unwise and proceeds from a failure to recognize and accept inescapable limitations on human agency. Yet most of us, being less than ideally rational, persist in these self-defeating patterns of thought and behavior. We do not consistently heed, or do not fully internalize, the Stoic's cornerstone insight. As a result, we suffer needlessly. Often, we convince ourselves that our suffering comes at the hands of others, when, in fact, it is a consequence of our own failures of rationality and generally inadequate mental discipline.

Interpersonal Relations and Suffering

The realm of interpersonal relations may be the single most pervasive source of misery among otherwise healthy persons. It may also be the area in which Stoic counsel is both most useful and most frequently flouted or forgotten. We ignore wise counsel at our peril. How much suffering would be averted by conscientious and consistent adherence to Marcus Aurelius' advice to himself in the arena of interpersonal endeavor? In the first entry in Book II of the *Meditations* Marcus enjoins himself to:

Begin each day by telling yourself: Today I shall be meeting with interference, ingratitude, insolence, disloyalty, ill-will, and selfishness – all of them due to the offenders' ignorance of what is good or evil. But for my part I have long perceived the nature of good and its nobility, the nature of evil and its meanness, and also the nature of the culprit himself, who is my brother (not in the physical sense, but as a fellow-creature similarly endowed with reason and a share of the divine); therefore none of those things can injure me, for nobody can implicate me in what is degrading. Neither can I be angry with my brother or fall foul of him; for he and I were born to work together, like a man's two hands, feet, or eyelids, or like the upper and lower rows of his teeth. To obstruct each other is against Nature's law – and what is irritation or aversion but a form of obstruction? [Book II, Section I]

In other words, Marcus admonishes himself to remember that the behavior, utterances, attitudes, and desires of persons other than himself all fall into the category of things that lie beyond his control. This reminder is to be repeated each and every day as preparation for the ubiquitous challenge presented by the encounter with one's fellows. He also tells himself that it is "contrary to nature" that he should become angry, offended, or jaundiced by another person's unwise or inappropriate behavior. He entrusts "Nature" (or, perhaps, its author) with a just ordering of all that which lies beyond his control, and reminds himself that aversion to the unfolding of the surrounding world is "against Nature's Law."

This daily recital distinguishing an area over which he believes himself to have direct control (i.e. some of his mental states), from an area that is clearly beyond his control (i.e. the thoughts and actions of other persons), is the psychological equivalent of girding himself with armor and shield before sallying forth into battle. It is intended to serve as deflection and defense against "blows" both expected and unforeseen. Marcus Aurelius understood the value of advance preparation in the face of inevitable challenges posed by interaction with our all-too-human brethren.

Unlike Garcin in Sartre's *No Exit*, who reaches the pessimistic conclusion that, "Hell is – other people," a committed and conscientious Stoic trains himself to "bear and forbear" in his dealings with his neighbor and brother (and we moderns would do well to add "sisters" also). Epictetus would insist that anyone who experiences other people as "hellish" must be confused as to what is properly "his concern" and within the control of his own will. When an agent's desire takes as its object anything that does not conform to the agent's will, the stage is set for disappointment and frustration, and needless conflict. It is irrational and unhealthy to allow oneself to become upset by things that other people say, think, and do. One simply cannot control such matters.

Insult and Offense

Consider the common phenomenon of the insult. An insult can have no power to traumatize with which its object does not endow it. One cannot control what others say, write, or think about oneself, and one cannot control the way in which anything said or written about oneself is received by those (other than, perhaps, oneself) who encounter such claims. It is, therefore, pointless and unwise to allow oneself to become enraged, offended or, in any way, to concern oneself with such matters. Slanders may damage one's reputation, jeopardize one's career, and undermine one's interpersonal relations in any number of ways. These, however, are also beyond one's direct control. If one's contentment depends upon states of affairs that do not conform to one's will, then one is virtually assured of irritation, disappointment, anxiety, and unease. Only through the extirpation of all attachment to those things that do not directly conform to the exertion of one's will can one maintain soundness of mind irrespective of the utterances, attitudes, and actions of persons other than oneself. Sticks and stones may assuredly break our bones, but neither spoken nor written word can ever hurt us if we develop an impregnable indifference to events and phenomena that we cannot command. All of us would do well to regularly remind ourselves to focus our efforts on self-discipline and self-improvement rather than wasting energy in worrying about how we are perceived by others.

Stoicism and Exertion

None of the foregoing entails a life of inactivity or withdrawal from social interaction. Active engagement in interpersonal relations and group efforts is, by no means, prohibited to the fully committed Stoic. To remain imperturbable in the face of interpersonal friction, one must simply learn to carefully and consistently distinguish between that part of the interaction that is "one's own" and the part that is determined by forces beyond one's control. One must assess success or failure solely by reference to one's self-control (or lack thereof). In the *Discourses*, Epictetus opens his commentary "On Anxiety" with the following:

> When I see anyone anxious, I say, what does this man want? Unless he wanted something or other not in his own power, how could he still be anxious? A musician, for instance, feels no anxiety while he is singing by himself; but when he appears upon the stage he does, even if his voice be ever so good, or he plays ever so well. For what he wishes is not only to sing well, but likewise to gain applause. But this is not in his own power.

And later:

> If, then, the things independent of our will are neither good nor evil, and all things that do depend on will are in our own power, and can neither be taken away from us nor given to us unless we please, what room is there left for anxiety? But we are anxious about this paltry body or estate of ours, or about what Caesar thinks, and not at all about anything internal... When, therefore, you see anyone pale with anxiety, just as the physician pronounces from the complexion that such a patient is disordered in the spleen, and another in the liver, so do you likewise say, this man is disordered in his desires

and aversions; he cannot walk steadily; he is in a fever. [Book II]

The musician suffers anxiety and worry only insofar as he desires that the audience should react to his performance in a particular fashion, or that he should be received positively. Were he sufficiently disciplined and devoid of all concern for things he cannot control, then any potential anxiety attached to his audience and their evaluation of him would be dissipated. The sage performer could still endeavor to give the best performance of which he is, on that occasion, capable – but the exertion of the effort to do so conforms entirely to the performer's will alone. Though his voice may crack, or his lungs may fail his will, the disciplined performer can remain unperturbed by any such happenstance and rest content in the knowledge that he has done the best that he is able. A recalcitrant body or inhospitable audience will not trouble the performer who understands that such matters lie beyond his control and should, therefore, be regarded as nothing of significance and unworthy of his concern. And all of us are, in some sense, performers of our respective roles – as Epictetus reminds us:

> Remember that you are an actor in a play the character of which is determined by the author – if short, then in a short one; if long, then in a long one. If it be his pleasure that you should enact a poor man, see that you act it well; or a cripple, or a ruler, or a private citizen. For this is your business, to act well the given part; but to choose it, belongs to God. [*Enchiridion*, 17]

One succeeds insofar as one does the best that one can given the circumstances and one's innate ability. Whether anyone else regards the effort as a success is immaterial to the rational man. Others will think what they will, and the surrounding world will unfold in accordance with God's plan. All of that is "not properly our own affair."

What's Love Got To Do With It?

Perhaps Stoicism offers reasonable advice about dealing with potentially damaging reactive attitudes such as anger, fear, anxiety, or frustration that may be triggered by interpersonal relationships, but what does it have to say about emotions generally deemed beneficial and valuable to the person who experiences them? What does Stoicism tell us, for example, about love? In remaining indifferent to "externals," must the committed Stoic deprive himself of experiences such as reciprocal love of spouse, children, and friends? If so, is this not sufficient reason to reject Stoic counsel – at least as it pertains to interpersonal relations? Surely, love is good. If Stoicism counsels us to regard love and loving relationships with indifference, well then so much the worse for Stoicism.

Lawrence Becker addresses this line of objection as part of his overall defense of a Stoic worldview and account of the virtuous life. In *A New Stoicism*, Becker points out that Stoics need not live a life devoid of the benefits of familial love and of friendship. Rather, the Stoic will rationally direct his will in such matters. Where and when it is reasonable to do so, the Stoic can both love and be loved:

> We simply hold that it is wise to calibrate the strength, depth, and dissemination of our attachments to the fragility and transience of the objects involved. (The ancients were fond of expressing this in terms of the distinction between things that are within our control, or are "up to us," and those that are not. But this is misleading)... That means we are very reluctant to endorse any attachment that is maximally strong, deep, and disseminated. It does not mean, however, that we endorse only weak, superficial attachments. On the

contrary, strong and deep attachments can be so encapsulated (undisseminated) in our personalities that we can continue to exercise our agency despite their rupture. (One child is dead, and another needs rescue. Parents who can rescue the living child despite the loss of the other have encapsulated attachments, nonetheless strong or deep – and we add virtuous – for being so.) [1998, p. 100]

So, rational love is an expression of the virtuous, well-ordered mind. But love for others must be tempered by recognition of human frailty and a rational understanding of the loved one's susceptibility to danger. The Stoic sage loves others, but also recognizes the mortality of his beloved. Both his own fate and that of his beloved are entrusted to providence insofar as "externals" are concerned, and the rational man is prepared to embrace and accept eventualities as they may arise.

Note

1. See, for example, Long (1971) and Botros (1985).

Death: A Propitious Misfortune

As early as Thales, philosophers have argued that death is nothing to fear because the dead no longer exist and, therefore, cannot suffer or be harmed. This position has had its detractors through the ages, and they have argued in various ways that death must be regarded as a misfortune. After all, death ends life and any of its attendant benefits. I will defend neither point of view. Instead, I will offer an account of the relationship between life and death intended to dilute the force of the view that death is a misfortune. In particular, I will argue that if death is a misfortune at all, it falls into a class of misfortunes that can only be suffered by those who have received a prior unearned benefit. I will call these *propitious misfortunes*. Death should be regarded as a propitious misfortune because it befalls only those fortunate enough to have been afforded the opportunity to exist in the first place. This may seem a trivial point, but it is not; if human life is a propitious phenomenon, this fact should not be trivialized or ignored in debates concerning the appropriate attitude toward death. The misfortune of death (if it is a misfortune) becomes much more palatable when it is balanced against the immense good fortune underlying the existence that it brings to an end.

Life and Death

There is something miraculous about human existence. This is either literally or figuratively the case. If there is a God, a designer of the universe and all that is in it, then human existence is literally a miracle. It is the product of divine intervention or, at least, divine design and intention. We are here because God decreed that it be so ("Let there be light!" and all that follows).

If, on the other hand, there is no God, no designer, no deity of any kind, and if the existence of human life is, at root, the product of brute, unguided forces of nature, then our presence in the universe is a statistical marvel. Our existence is miraculous in the non-literal sense in which (say) multiple successive lottery wins would count as miraculous. If anyone balks at this loose use of the term "miraculous," perhaps "astronomically lucky" would serve as an adequate substitute.

It is against this backdrop of the miraculous (or, at least, the *astronomically lucky*) character of our existence that I wish to explore the nature of death and its relationship to life. If life is a necessary prerequisite for death, and life is an unearned benefit of the highest order, then we must take our good fortune into account as we evaluate the alleged misfortune of death. If death can be coherently deemed a misfortune at all, this misfortune must be balanced against the weight of the good fortune that necessarily precedes it. Death can be a misfortune only in roughly the same sense as (say) the tax payment that accompanies a lottery win. In each case, the "burden" falls only upon those previously afforded an unearned benefit.

Epicurus is probably the best-known (though not the earliest) defender of the position that death cannot be a misfortune, because the dead no longer exist, and if one does not exist, one cannot suffer or be damaged. Those antagonistic to this position have subsequently raised a variety of objections claiming that an individual can indeed suffer a misfortune (or an evil) as a result of her death. The Epicurean tradition has, of course, raised its counter-objections through the ages, and these have been designed to prove that only a misunderstanding of the true nature of death could account for the view that one's death can be a misfortune for oneself. So goes the debate, and it continues to this day.

Perhaps the most common claim made against the Epicurean attitude toward death is that it fails to recognize the fact that death deprives the individual of future experiences that would have occurred had the individual's death not intervened. One's death deprives one of one's future life experiences, and it is this fact that (at least in most cases) constitutes the misfortune that is associated with death.

The Argument From Deprivation

The standard argument for this position runs roughly as follows:

1. If S dies, then S is thereby deprived of all future experiences.
2. If S's future experiences would have had overall positive value for S, then S's death deprives S of that positive value.
3. If S is deprived of positive value, then S suffers a misfortune.

----

4. Therefore, if S dies, then S thereby suffers a misfortune (at least in those cases in which S's future would have had overall positive value for S).

Hence Thomas Nagel claims that death, if it is an evil at all, can be so "only because of what it deprives us of." Don Marquis, in "Why Abortion Is Immoral," argues that the termination of the life of the fetus deprives it of its future experiences, and it is for this reason that abortion is (perhaps with special exceptions) immoral – it imposes an undeserved misfortune upon the fetus. Fred Feldman, in "Some Puzzles About the Evil of Death," argues that an individual's death is, at least in some cases, an evil insofar as it is an event in the actual world such that the nearest possible world in which it does not happen is a world with greater overall positive value for the individual in question. In other words, Feldman claims that death is an evil insofar as it deprives us of positive experiences that we would have had had we not died just then.

In making this case, Feldman develops a rough system for quantifying an individual's welfare level in different possible worlds, and compares a possible world in which he dies in an airplane crash to the next nearest possible world in which he does not. He claims that:

> ... my death would be bad for me not because it would cause me to suffer pain, and not because it would itself be intrinsically bad for me. Rather, it would be bad for me because it would deprive me of 600 units of pleasure that I would have had if it had not happened when it did. More precisely, it would be bad for me because my welfare level at the nearest world where it occurs is 600 points lower than my welfare level at the nearest world where it does not occur.

So, Feldman offers a perspicuous presentation of (probably) the most common view about death as a misfortune. Death is an evil because it deprives one of the life experience that one would otherwise have had. But if death does constitute deprivation, it can deprive us only of the goods or benefits associated with life. Life itself, however, is something of a lottery, and only the "lottery winners" can suffer the misfortune of death.

The Evolution and Birth Lotteries

Let us suppose that there is no God, no deity, no designer of the universe. If organic life is the outcome of an unguided process of evolution, then the existence of the human species is a propitious accident (for *humans* anyway). This assumes, of course, that the existence of a particular species constitutes a positive (overall) value *for* members of that species. Each of us is fortunate that our species, the biological type of thing that we are, came into existence. It might not have. We are all, therefore, fortunate that the wildly improbable appearance of the human species has actually, against all odds, occurred.

In addition to this good fortune, however, there is the additional stroke of (apparently monumental) luck, for each individual member of the species, that *that particular* individual came to exist. This assumes, of course, that the existence of each individual member, H_i, of the human species, constitutes a positive (overall) value *for* H_i. That is, I am assuming that (for example) my existence constitutes a positive (overall) value *for me*.

It is as if each of us has won two separate lotteries. The initial prize is shared with every other member of the species. The second "winning ticket" (so to speak) is the event of the particular individual's birth (or conception). Millions of distinct individuals, or no individuals at all, could result from any particular instance of human sexual union. On each such fertile occasion, millions of would-be individuals are *not* conceived. If conception occurs, only one (or, at most, a few) of those many potential individuals is afforded an opportunity at life. For any particular individual member of the human species, H_i, it is, therefore, a tremendous statistical improbability that H_i (as opposed to some other individual or none at all) comes to exist. Couple this with the improbability of the unguided evolution of the human species as a whole, and each particular one of us is revealed to be an astronomical improbability.

One might point out that some individuals, because their lives are (overall) negatively valuable to themselves, are not at all fortunate for having come to exist. Consider, for example, persons who live predominantly painful lives. One could, perhaps, make a plausible case that such persons experience lives that are not worth living. Such individuals may exist, but then it is not at all clear how their deaths could be misfortunes for them. When they die, they are released from suffering and "deprived" only of a future that is not worth having (or so one might argue). The same claim could be generalized to the human species as a whole (by a sufficiently Schopenhauerian type of philosopher). Perhaps all human life is predominantly misery. But again, if that is so, then it is difficult to see the misfortune in the mortality of the species as a whole, or of any particular individual. The point is this: one's death can be a misfortune only if one's life is (on balance) *a good*. An existence worth having is an unearned good (no one *earns* existence) and, in the absence of a designer, constitutes a propitious phenomenon or accident.

The Creation Lottery

If, on the other hand, there is a God who designed the universe, brought it into being, and guides its progress, then we (as a species and as individuals) exist only by leave of the divine will. Death is then part of the same design that permits each life. Presumably, there are indefinitely many possible design plans that could have been actualized by the creator. It seems likely that, of all possible worlds, most lack human life altogether. It also seems likely that, of all possible worlds containing human life in general, most lack any particular individual who appears in the actual world. In other words, most possible worlds do not have "us" (either collectively or individually) in them. Therefore, each of us is tremendously fortunate that: 1) the evolution of the human species is part of the creator's chosen design plan, and 2) we, as particular individuals, are part of the human species within the chosen design plan. If there is a divine creator, then all of the world is "God's stage," and each of us "actors" is providentially conjured into existence and afforded an (unearned) opportunity to perform a role in the master's play. Unfortunately, however, God has scripted a play in which each performer runs out of lines before the final curtain.

Perhaps it is, in some sense, true that one suffers a misfortune when one's time on stage is ended. Perhaps the misfortune is still greater if one "gets the hook" unexpectedly or after only a few moments in the production. In any case, only those fortunate enough to have been scripted into the great play must suffer the misfortune in question. Many would-be actors never get their chance at all, but instead remain mere character sketches forever confined to God's "unpublished works." Only those who have been fortunate enough to "fit the script" ever get cast as living, breathing characters. Eventually, these characters live and breathe no more, but we must remember that God might have written any of (presumably) infinitely many other scripts in which we never would have appeared. In fact, it may not be necessary that God produces any script at all. We are fortunate that there is something rather than nothing, and that we are part of the something that exists.

Perhaps, as Leibniz suggests, God necessarily creates precisely this world because it is the best of all possibilities. If so, then each of us is very fortunate that the best of all possible worlds requires our existence (collectively as well as individually). It should also be noted that if this is the case, then the best of all possible worlds comes complete with our death (collectively as well as individually) scripted into it. The persons (or potential persons) in all other than the best of all possible worlds never have to die, but neither do they ever get the chance to live.

Again, the point is that death can be a suffered misfortune (if at all) only for those fortunate enough to have been given a chance at life in the first place. Life – mine, yours, and "ours" collectively – is either a propitious accident on the grandest order of improbability, or it is a gift of supernatural proportion for which we owe immeasurable gratitude. We either receive life as a gift from on high, or our astoundingly unlikely phylogeny emerges out of a primordial ooze, and then this improbable event is (more or less) recapitulated in the ontogeny of each individual one of us. The whole of life is either miraculous, or it is a stroke (or series of strokes) of almost unimaginable good fortune. And then we drop dead.

Death and Taxes: Some Analogies

One might argue that even a lottery winner can suffer a misfortune and does so when the tax is levied against her winnings. We can even imagine a system of taxation in which that misfortune is magnified. Imagine a world in which lottery winners are allowed to enjoy their winnings for an unspecified amount of time, but are then forced to return, without warning, the entire unused portion to the state. Having one's winnings forcibly taken away arguably constitutes a misfortune even if the windfall is neither earned nor deserved. A lottery winner is deprived of the positive value derived from her winnings when the state takes it back. As Feldman might put it, the possible world in which a lottery winner is taxed has a welfare level lower than the nearest possible world in which that lottery winner is not taxed. Granted. But we miss something crucial when we fail to note that *only lottery winners* have to suffer this particular misfortune. It is, therefore, a *propitious misfortune*. The prerequisite for suffering this particular type of misfortune is the prior receipt of a benefit that is, itself, unearned. Those who do not win the lottery do not suffer the added tax, but they also do not win the lottery!

Perhaps a better analogy could be drawn to a lottery among a very large population of prisoners. Suppose that there are billions and billions of them. Suppose further that a small subgroup of these prisoners will be chosen, either at random or by the warden's whim (not on the basis of merit), to be freed for an unspecified length of time. When their time on the outside is up, they will be (infallibly) recaptured and sent back to prison. There will be no warning as to this impending end to their freedom. Recapture is, at least arguably, a misfortune, but only those fortunate enough to have been freed in the first place are ever subjected to recapture. Such recapture is a propitious misfortune insofar as it is suffered by only a select, fortunate few.

Similarly, if death is a misfortune at all, it can be so only for those who have previously claimed the wildly improbable benefit of existence against all odds. Only those who win the "birth lottery" (not to mention the prior "evolutionary lottery" that allowed the species to exist) are "saddled" with the misfortune

75

of death. So, lamenting the fact that one is not immortal is a bit like lamenting the fact that one must eventually give back the remainder of one's lottery winnings. It is, perhaps, even more like a freed prisoner, who has done nothing to earn his liberty, lamenting the fact that his freedom will not last forever.

One should, I suggest, have the attitude toward one's impending death that one would deem appropriate toward the impending return of one's lottery winnings, or toward the impending return to incarceration while one enjoys the freedman's sojourn outside the prison walls. Assuming that there is no afterlife, we shall eventually return to nothingness (we know not when). This misfortune (if it is one) is substantially more palatable when it is balanced against the weight of the good fortune that is its prerequisite. This is the character of a propitious misfortune. Paradoxical as it may seem, we all have the good fortune to be in a position to die some day. To parody Tennyson, 'tis (at least in most cases) better to have lived and lost, than never to have lived at all.

Roman Buddha

Those who teach a Dhamma for the abandoning of passion, for the abandoning of aversion, for the abandoning of delusion – their Dhamma is well-taught.
– Ājīvaka Sutta [AN 3:72]

Rudyard Kipling tells us that, "East is East and West is West and never the twain shall meet." To some this may seem an apt summation of the intellectual and spiritual chasm yawning between the dominant wisdom traditions originating respectively in certain areas of Asia and in the early Mediterranean city-states that spawned Western culture. The multifarious strands of Buddhism (and other Asian wisdom traditions) are often regarded as too esoteric and culturally alien for the earthy pragmatism of the industrial West and its predominantly materialistic worldview. The admonitions of the Noble Eightfold Path are all well and good for tonsured monks swaddled in flowing robes, or cave-dwelling hermits perched in the lotus position on some Himalayan mountaintop, contemplatively indifferent to "worldly" concerns, but what has all that got to do with life in the "real world" of career, family, financial obligations, and material need? I argue that the Roman Stoic philosopher Epictetus (55–135 CE) offered practical counsel through which the West may begin to more comfortably approach Buddhism as a system of self-governance and path to awakening. Epictetus' collected *Discourses* and *Enchiridion* offer glimpses of a spirit which Buddhist practitioners will, I think, find strikingly kindred.

The West has produced intellectuals of the order of Newton and Einstein, statesmen like Churchill, and captains of industry like the Rockefellers and Bill Gates – but what are we to do with Bodhisattvas, lamas, rinpoches, and the rest? It all seems so...

"Oriental." Those Westerners on the religious quest are likely to be drawn to familiar Abrahamic traditions and have no need of exotic spirituality wafting in from the East. Furthermore, the Eastern sages seem, until recently perhaps, to have been in no particular hurry to illumine the barbarian West. There are few reports of Bodhisattvas reincarnating in this part of the world – and if one did, no one would pay much attention (with the possible exception of a few aging hippies and maybe Richard Gere). What inspires "them" is just not going to fly for "us" – and vice versa. There is a fundamental incommensurability in these competing conceptions of the human condition separating Eastern and Western approaches to the "good life." We should not expect to find large tracts of common ground on which "the twain" may meet to share the wisdom of their respective sages. So goes an all-too-common misconception on both sides of the putative divide.

Slave and Sage

This kind of parochialism is misleading, oversimplified, and paints the relevant cultural traditions in overly stark contrast. The West has, I would argue, produced its fair share of (arguably) enlightened beings and, in at least a few instances, they have significantly influenced the evolution and development of Western culture. Socrates, Jesus and Mohammed have obviously left their marks and exhorted billions to reconsider the human condition, our relationship to the transcendent, our values, and our way of life. I would like to suggest, however, that a much lesser known and insufficiently appreciated figure may be our best hope for finding a worldview within which East and West might encounter each other in a light more felicitous to mutual understanding and appreciation. Just as it is instructive and valuable for Westerners to develop an understanding and appreciation of Buddhism and other strands of Asian philosophy and/or religion, so too is it worthwhile for Buddhists and practitioners of allied Eastern wisdom traditions to become better acquainted with like-minded intellects that contributed to the philosophical, cultural, and religious foundations of the Western world. In addition to the aforementioned figures of indisputable historic and cultural interest, one sage of the Roman Empire stands out for special (and long overdue) attention. The Roman Stoic, Epictetus, may serve as a valuable nexus through which the Buddha's wisdom could be rendered more accessible to those reared outside of an Asian cultural context. Also, a clearer understanding of practical therapeutic philosophy as developed in the ancient West may be brought to the attention of Eastern practitioners through an exploration of the methods and application of Epictetan counsel. Certainly, in my own case, it was an appreciation of Stoicism and the wisdom of Epictetus, in particular, that opened the door to Buddhism and eased those first tentative steps toward concepts such as impermanence, renunciation, and a synoptic ethic of mental discipline. Perhaps, given a bit of luck and intrepidity, fellow seekers from East and West may encounter each other and develop a richer understanding of commonalities intersecting their respective traditions and spiritual heritage.

Epictetus was born a slave but ultimately became an influential teacher and philosopher whose advocacy of Stoicism had a tremendous impact on Roman culture and subsequent developments – Christianity among them. Prince Siddhartha Gautama enjoyed the material benefits of aristocratic birth but opted for a wandering homeless life, the pursuit of wisdom and mental discipline, and became, of course, one of the most influential spiritual figures in world history. The two could hardly have begun their lives in more disparate circumstances, yet Epictetus, and the man who would become known to posterity as the Buddha, arrived at very much the same understanding of the human condition and its fundamental challenges. Both keenly understood the dangers of psychological and emotional attachment to the uncontrollable vicissitudes of human experience. Both counselled renunciation of the usual worldly desires for fortune, fame, and self-aggrandizing power. Both maintained that true liberty is won through thoughtful discipline, proper conduct, and a deep, penetrating understanding of the nature of reality and one's place within it. Though advancing somewhat different metaphysical accounts of persons and the ultimate nature of their relationship to surrounding reality, the Eastern sage and his Western counterpart both offered very similar practical programs of therapeutic guidance for the attainment of liberation from the common ills and dissatisfactions endemic to humanity.

Epictetan Dharma

Most people live as slaves – not in the sense in which Epictetus was literally another man's property, but in the sense that they allow their emotional well-being to depend upon conditions over which they themselves have no ultimate control. They enslave themselves through irrationality, ignorance and indiscipline. Their desires are often unhealthy, unwise and all too often lead to self-destruction (to say nothing of their unfortunate impact upon others). The common result of unfulfilled desire is anger, frustration, anxiety, dissatisfaction, or what the Buddha might have called a pervasive dukkha. In the *Discourses*, we find Epictetus instructing his students to pay careful attention to craving, its causes and, perhaps most importantly, its likely consequences:

There are three fields of study, in which he who would be wise and good must be exercised: that of the desires and aversions, that he may not be disappointed of the one, nor incur the other; that of the pursuits and avoidances, and, in general, the duties of life, that he may act with order and consideration, and not carelessly; the third includes integrity of mind and prudence, and, in general, whatever belongs to the judgment.

Of these points the principal and most urgent is that which reaches the passions; for passion is only produced by a disappointment of one's desires and an incurring of one's aversions. It is this which introduces perturbations, tumults, misfortunes, and calamities; this is the spring of sorrow, lamentation, and envy; this renders us envious and emulous, and incapable of hearing reason. [Book III, Ch. Two]

Epictetus also advises careful and consistent observation of the crucial distinction between that which conforms directly to the exertion of the will and that which depends upon factors external to the agent's unmediated direction. Wise persons rationally control that which is within their power and remain placidly indifferent to conditions over which they have no direct influence. In so doing, the wise remain untroubled by the uncontrollable unfolding of reality, and never experience frustrated desire. They want only that which they have the power to produce and are averse only to that which they have the power to avoid. All else is accepted and embraced simply as it is:

There are things which are within our power, and there are things which are beyond our power. Within our power are opinion, aim, desire, aversion, and, in one word, whatever affairs are our own. Beyond our power are body, property, reputation, office, and, in one word, whatever are not properly our own affairs.

Now, the things within our power are by nature free, unrestricted, unhindered; but those beyond our power are weak, dependent, restricted, alien. Remember, then, that if you attribute freedom to things by nature dependent, and take what belongs to others for your own, you will be hindered, you will lament, you will be disturbed, you will find fault both with gods and men. But if you take for your own only that which is your own, and view what belongs to others just as it really is, then no one will ever compel you, no one will restrict you, you will find fault with no one, you will accuse no one, you will do nothing against your will; no one will hurt you, you will not have an enemy, nor will you suffer any harm. [*Enchiridion*, I]

The wise suffer no real harm because they understand that the only real harm is that to which one subjects oneself through irrational attachment. All other states of affairs are embraced, welcomed, and rendered impotent to disrupt the deep, abiding serenity born of careful attention and wise discernment. In another passage from the *Discourses*, we notice Epictetus describing the condition of the "good man" in terms that call to mind the Buddhist account of the arahant or the awakened practitioner:

A good man is invincible; for he does not contend where he is not superior. If you would have his land, take it; take his servants, take his office, take his body. But you will never frustrate his desire, nor make him incur his aversion. He engages in no combat but what concerns objectives within his own control. How then can he fail to be invincible? [Book III, Ch. Six]

Consider how closely this resembles the Buddha's remarks concerning the equanimity of those who have conquered desire and illusion. In Bhikkhu Bodhi's recent anthology, *In the Buddha's Words*, we find these thoughts from the Dhātuvibhanga Sutta regarding the aspiring arahant:

He does not construct or generate any volition tending toward either existence or non-existence. Since he does not construct or generate any volition tending toward either existence or non-existence, he does not cling to anything in this world. Not clinging, he is not agitated. Not being agitated, he personally attains Nibbāna. [2005, p. 410; from MN 140: III 244–47]

The fruits of this mental discipline are release and equanimity:

He indeed is the all-vanquishing sage,
The one released from all the knots
Who has reached the supreme state of peace,
Nibbāna, without fear from any side. [p. 422; from AN 4:23; II 23–24 – It 112; 121–23]

We see that both wise men hold out the prospect of imperturbability for those who renounce transient worldly attainments and devote themselves instead to mental discipline and the extirpation of unhealthy desire, aversion and attachment. Only through turning inward and learning to govern the unruly mind and its passions may one hope to attain true wisdom and the spiritual "invincibility" of the "all-vanquishing sage."

Similarly, we need only compare a passage from *The Dhammapada* with a nugget of Epictetan counsel from the *Enchiridion*, or *Handbook*, to perceive a deep confluence of the flowing streams of Buddhist and Stoic wisdom regarding the renunciation of ill-will and hatred as crucial to the attainment of peace within a well-disciplined mind:

"He abused me, he beat me, he defeated me, he robbed me": the hatred of those who harbour such thoughts is not appeased. [*Dhammapada*, 3]

Were it not for the citations, one would be hard-pressed to discern which remark had been uttered by the Roman Stoic and which originated with the Buddha:

> Remember that it is not he who gives abuse or blows who insults; but the view we take of these things as insulting. When, therefore, anyone provokes you, be assured that it is your own opinion which provokes you. Try, therefore, in the first place, not to be bewildered by appearances. For if you once gain time and respite, you will more easily command yourself. [*Enchiridion*, 20]

Is not essentially the same truth offered in both these passages? For all practical purposes, the Epictetan attitude to insult, offence and the like is indistinguishable from the Buddhist admonition to renounce unskillful thoughts such as hatred and anger.

Divergence and Confluence

For those who would focus on differences between Stoic and Buddhist metaphysics insofar as the two apparently diverge concerning issues such as the ontological fundamentality of impermanence, it may be instructive to note that remarks very reminiscent of the Buddha's appear throughout Epictetus' advice to his students regarding the insignificance of ephemeral states of affairs. Both men clearly understand the pitfalls of devotion to impermanent conditions and the liberation available to those who are able to renounce them. In a section offering advice for the attainment of tranquility, the *Discourses* remind us to:

> Remember that it is not only the desire of riches and power that debases us and subjects us to others, but even the desire of quiet, leisure, learning, or travelling. For, in general, reverence for any external thing whatever makes us subject to others... Nothing is so essential to prosperity as that it should be permanent and unhindered. [Book IV, Ch. Four]

Epictetus also denigrates the common obsession with the body and its accouterments as well as the usual assumption that the body constitutes "the self" or is, at least, indispensable to one's well-being:

> When you would have your body perfect, is it in your own power, or is it not? "It is not." When you would be healthy? "It is not." When you would be handsome? "It is not." When you would live or die? "It is not." Body then is not our own; but is subject to everything that proves stronger than itself... Is despising death, then, an action in our power, or is it not? "It is."... You ought to consider your whole body as a useful ass, with a pack-saddle on, so long as possible, so long as it is allowed. But if there should come a military conscription, and a soldier should lay hold on it, let it go. Do not resist, or murmur; otherwise you will be first beaten and lose the ass after all. And since you are thus to regard even the body itself, think what remains to do concerning things to be provided for the sake of the body. If that be an ass, the rest are but bridles, pack-saddles, shoes, oats, hay for him. Let these go too. Quit them yet more easily and expeditiously. [Book IV, Ch. One]

Do these passages not ring harmonious with the Buddha's admonition to relinquish the emotional stranglehold on conditioned phenomena and self-centered desire? Bhikkhu Bodhi presents this passage from the Samyutta Nikāya:

> Suppose, monks, a dog tied up on a leash was bound to a strong post or pillar: it would just keep on running and revolving around that same post or pillar. So too, the uninstructed worldling regards form as self... feeling as self... perception as self... volitional formations as self... consciousness as self... He just keeps running and revolving around form,

around feeling, around perception, around volitional formations, around consciousness. As he keeps on running and revolving around them, he is not freed from form, not freed from feeling, not freed from perception, not freed from volitional formations, not freed from consciousness. He is not freed from birth, aging, and death; not freed from sorrow, lamentation, pain, dejection, and despair; not freed from suffering, I say. [2005, pp. 39–40; SN 22:99]

Such comparisons could assuredly continue and would address numerous points of intersection common to the practical counsel offered by these two sages of the ancient world. Let us, however, explore a further crucial confluence that may be overlooked due to a common misinterpretation of the Buddha's attitude toward desire. While some may claim that the Buddha advised the complete renunciation of all desire, whereas Epictetus did not, it turns out, upon closer inspection, that Epictetan and Buddhist analyses of the propriety and value of desire and its many possible objects are far more similar than one might initially suppose.

Governing Desire

Students in introductory courses on Western philosophy and philosophy of religion often respond incredulously to the suggestion that enlightenment, according to the Buddha, requires the renunciation of desire. They tend to be, in the first place, very skeptical that mere mortals could possibly extirpate all desire but, more importantly, many question the wisdom and, indeed, the desirability of attaining this condition of desirelessness. What kind of life, they wonder indignantly, would that be? Wouldn't an "enlightened" life be sedentary, boring, vapid, and without purpose? Buddhist practice may be valuable for dealing with life's difficulties and reducing our suffering, but surely we should not completely extinguish all desire. Many of our desires, they insist, are healthy, invigorating, and imbue our endeavors with meaning and purpose. Does the Buddha really counsel the renunciation of all forms of desire, they wonder? If so, he advocates an anemic lifelessness and retreat into emotional isolation, rather than a real, full-blooded engagement with reality and our fellow human beings. Far from being a path to awakening, Buddhism, it seems to many Western students, offers to put us to sleep. This, however, is a misunderstanding of the Buddha's analysis of desire – one that may be clarified with a bit of help from Epictetus' counsel regarding the proper management of desire and aversion from the Stoic perspective.

The Desire to Extirpate Desire

In "Three Cheers for Taṇhā," Robert Morrison (Dharmachārin Sāgaramati) seeks to dispel some common misconceptions about the Buddha's analysis of taṇhā and the skillful response to this condition of unenlightened existence. According to Morrison, taṇhā should be understood as:

> ... a metaphor that evokes the general condition that all unenlightened beings find themselves in in the world: a state of being characterized by "thirst" that compels a pursuit for appeasement, the urge to seek out some form of gratification. [2008]

The general condition of unenlightened existence is dukkha or dissatisfaction because impermanent states of affairs do not allow for a permanent slaking of the common "thirst" for sensual gratification and pleasurable experience. New "thirsts" arise and old ones reassert themselves after relatively brief periods of abatement. Taṇhā itself, however, does not lead irretrievably to dukkha. Taṇhā can inspire skillful (kusala) effort as well as unskillful (akusala) floundering. So, we see that the real culprits are grasping, clinging and aversion regarding impermanent states that cause various forms of pleasure and/or displeasure. The extirpation of dukkha, or dissatisfaction, is not quite the same thing as, and does not necessarily require, the extirpation of all desire. We eliminate dukkha by learning to deal skillfully with our mental states and habits of cognition. We pay attention to the nature of mental states, the conditions of their arising, and their relation to subsequent unsatisfactory states of being. Aversion and desire regarding uncontrollable elements of one's environment, other people, socio-political conditions, etc. – these invite dukkha because such conditions need not satisfy our desires and may incur our aversions. Aversion to conducting oneself in unwise or unskillful fashion, or the desire to improve one's understanding and mental discipline, or to assist others in their attempts to improve – these are neither unhealthy nor inappropriate because one's efforts in these areas do conform to one's properly disciplined will.

Skillful and Unskillful Cognition

Morrison again points to the distinction between tanhā as a general condition of unenlightened existence and skillful or unskillful methods of dealing with this condition:

> For example, if a heterosexual man encounters a very attractive woman, this will probably give rise to a pleasurable "feeling-sensation", which in turn can form the condition for the arising of affects such as "lust" [rāga], "infatuation" [pema], etc. Whereas, if we encounter someone who tells us that we are stupid, then the "feeling-sensation" is more likely to be unpleasant, which in turn can form the condition for the arising of affects such as "aversion" [paṭigha] or "hatred" [dosa], etc. The response to "feeling-sensation" is going to be a particular affect, and tanhā here, as I suggest, is not so much a particular affect, but is best understood metaphorically, as a general condition from which there can arise all manner of

affects, including, as we shall see, what Buddhism regards as "skillful" (kusala) affects, the kind of affects cultivated in an active spiritual life. [2008]

Gautama's skillful understanding of, and encounters with, taṇhā precipitated a spiritual search for liberation from the ills of unenlightened existence – a search culminating in his emergence as the man historically revered as the Buddha. Unskillful understanding of, or encounter with, taṇhā takes as its object some impermanent condition over which one has no direct control and, therefore, leads to further dukkha. Skillfulness with respect to taṇhā, however, takes as its object conditions that one can control, such as the renunciation of unwholesome attachments, and the directing of one's mental energies so as to realize peace and equanimity.

The Buddha carefully distinguished skillful from unskillful cognition, habit, and behavior. He did not simply condemn all experience of taṇhā irrespective of context or consequences. If an encounter with taṇhā does not generate dukkha or, moreover, actually facilitates the diminution of dukkha, then that experience, and a skillful understanding of it, can be part of a noble search for liberation. In "Desire & Imagination in the Buddhist Path" Thanissaro Bhikkhu makes the point that the Buddha did not regard all desire as necessarily unskillful:

The notion of a skillful desire may sound strange, but a mature mind intuitively pursues the desires it sees as skillful and drops those it perceives as not. Basic in everyone is the desire for happiness. Every other desire is a strategy for attaining that happiness. You want an iPod, a sexual partner, or an experience of inner peace because you think it will make you happy. Because these secondary desires are strategies, they follow a pattern. They spring from an inchoate feeling of lack and limitation; they employ your powers of perception to identify the cause of the limitation; and they use your powers of creative imagination to conceive a solution to it.

But despite their common pattern, desires are not monolithic. Each offers a different perception of what's lacking in life, together with a different picture of what the solution should be. A desire for a sandwich comes from a perception of physical hunger and proposes to solve it with a Swiss-on-rye. A desire to climb a mountain focuses on a different set of hungers – for accomplishment, exhilaration, self-mastery – and appeals to a different image of satisfaction. Whatever the desire, if the solution actually leads to happiness, the desire is skillful. If it doesn't, it's not. However, what seems to be a skillful desire may lead only to a false or transitory happiness not worth the effort entailed. So wisdom starts as a meta-desire: to learn how to recognize skillful and unskillful desires for what they actually are. [2006 – emphasis added]

The wise skillfully investigate, monitor, and govern their desires, and the objects of those desires, in pursuit of liberation from the ills endemic to unenlightened existence. They do not reflexively repudiate all desire as unhealthy or inappropriate.

Stephen Ruppenthal makes a similar observation in his introduction to Chapter 24 of Eknath Easwaran's translation of *The Dhammapada*:

All the Buddha's teachings come round to this one practical point: to find permanent joy, we have to learn how not to yield to selfish desire.

This conclusion is so contrary to human nature that it is not surprising to hear even experts maintain that in preaching the extinction of desire, the Buddha was denying everything that makes life worth living. But trishna [taṇhā] does not mean all desire; it means selfish desire, the conditioned craving for self-aggrandizement... He distinguishes raw, unregulated, self-directed trishna from the unselfish and uplifting desire to dissolve one's egotism in selfless service of all. The person who makes no effort to go against the base craving for personal satisfaction is headed for more sorrow. [1985, p. 179 – emphasis and brackets added]

So, the effort to renounce "base craving" and selfish desire is skillful and should not be disparaged simply because such effort is linked with desire. Ruppenthal pointedly inquires how such intense effort could possibly be made without the inspiration of desire for liberation from the common dissatisfactions of the all-too-human condition. He then cites the Samyutta Nikāya in support of his contention that the Buddha's analysis identifies selfish desires as antecedents of dukkha, and actually extols the virtues of skillful usages of unselfish desire in generating and sustaining wholesome mental states. Here is one example of a passage Ruppenthal cites in support of his contention:

If, while holding on to concentration and one-pointedness of mind, one emphasizes desire, that is concentration of desire. One generates desire for the non-arising of unwholesome states that have not yet arisen; he puts forth effort and mobilizes energy... He generates desire for the arising of wholesome states that have not yet arisen; he puts forth effort and mobilizes energy. [Samyutta Nikāya, v, 268]

So, the desire for wholesome states, and behavior in accordance with that desire, is skillful, whereas selfish desire for sense pleasure and gratification is unskillful and this "kama-trishna" (kāma-taṇhā) is a causal antecedent of dukkha.

Skillful habits of mind and conduct tend toward satisfaction and equanimity whereas unskillfulness tends toward dissatisfaction, discontent, distress – dukkha. Buddhism's central focus is the understanding of dukkha, its nature, origin, and prescribed methods designed to bring about its cessation. If dukkha ensues from selfish desire, enlightenment requires an understanding of criteria by which one may identify and relinquish selfish desire, as well as an understanding of the means by which one may understand and engage in skillful cultivation of appropriate desires. What exactly, though, differentiates wise encounters with desire from the thoughtless selfishness that increases and exacerbates needless suffering?

Buddhist Skillfulness and Epictetan "Internals"

When it comes to desire and its objects, we tend to put the cart before the horse, so to speak. A self-centered desire forms, and we set about trying to bend conditions to the satisfaction of this desire. We try, in short, to make the world as we wish it to be. In doing so, we behave unskillfully. A recalcitrant world is apt to leave us unsatisfied. There is, I claim, a way to incorporate Epictetus' distinction between "internals" (or that which is "up to us") and "externals" (or that which is not "up to us") to clarify the Buddha's analysis of selfish desire (taṇhā) as distinct from a skillful understanding of, and encounter with, desire, aversion, and taṇhā as the pervasive condition in which the unenlightened find themselves. Selfish desire insists that the world conform to its dictates, whereas a skillful understanding of desire involves the mental effort to produce harmony between one's mental states and unalterable conditions of reality by deft alteration of the "internal" realm of cognition. In other words, selfish desire involves an insistence upon changing the world to suit one's whims, but skillfulness involves the effort to alter one's consciousness and attitudes so as to embrace conditions that simply lie beyond one's control. The Buddha and Epictetus both counselled mental discipline designed to reduce the needless suffering that inevitably results from ill-considered attitudes and desires. To insist that conditions of the "external" world must be thus or so, especially when one lacks the power to produce the desired conditions, virtually assures discontent. Epictetus instructs his students about how to approach circumstances in which they encounter the pull of desire, and reveals a method for dealing wisely with this ubiquitous challenge:

Why, what else but to distinguish between what is mine, and what not mine – what I can and what I cannot do? I must die; must I die groaning too? I must be exiled; does anyone keep me from going smiling and cheerful, and serene? "Betray a secret?" I will not betray it, for this is in my own power. "Then I will fetter you." What do you say, man? Fetter me? You will fetter my leg, but not even Zeus himself can get the better of my free will... These are the things that philosophers ought to study; these they ought daily to write, and in these exercise themselves. [*Discourses*, Book I, Ch. One]

For it makes no sense to "exercise" oneself concerning matters regarding which the strength of one's will has no purchase. It is wise to skillfully focus one's efforts upon that which lies within one's control, and to refrain from making demands upon, or hanging one's contentment upon, that which one cannot control by effort of will. Rather than allowing selfless desire to ensue from our careful investigations of reality, we typically form prescriptive desires that tacitly demand conformity of a world that is almost entirely beyond our control. Epictetus perceived the perils of frustrated desire and taught that one should only desire that which one has the power directly to produce without mediation or complicity from the external world. The rest of reality's unfolding, the "external" world, is to be embraced as it stands. The great Stoic, and one-time slave, counsels his students to:

Demand not that events should happen as you wish; but wish them to happen as they do happen, and your life will be serene. [*Enchiridion*, 8]

Note that this is not the expression of a simple, fatalistic attitude, but rather a counsel to develop the mental discipline necessary to maintaining serenity no matter how surrounding events may unfold. Epictetus counselled others, but did not allow his contentment to depend upon anyone adhering to his counsel. His efforts were his to control, but he could not produce the student's understanding or improvement by sheer force of his will. He regarded such states of affairs as "externals" and did not rely upon them to secure his happiness or contentment. There must be rational limitations on desire and/or attachment to the satisfaction thereof. This is essential to attaining tranquility irrespective of changing external circumstances.

Truth is, arguably, the sine qua non of skillfulness in matters of belief. Though much else may be said for a belief – that it is, for example, interesting, useful, comforting or pervasive – it is an epistemic failure insofar as it is untrue. The adoption of, or acquiescence in, false belief is not generally conducive to skillful interaction with the world because false beliefs do not, as it were, "fit" the world with which one is engaged.

Startlingly enough, the otherwise obvious implications of reality's independence from our mental states seems to elude many of us when it comes to propriety or skillfulness in matters of desire. We inveterately fall into the habit of attempting to force the world to satisfy our desires and suffer frustration, anger, and anxiety as a result of our inability to do so. It is as if we believe that we can force a "fit" between reality and our desires, even though we recognize the hopelessness of most attempts to force a similar "fit" with our beliefs. There is, I suspect, at least a flash of irony in John Searle's characterization of the difference between our general attitudes regarding the world's relationship to our beliefs as opposed to our desires:

> It is the aim of belief to be true, and to the extent that belief is true, it succeeds. To the extent that it is false, it fails. Desires,

on the other hand, are not supposed to represent how the world is, but how we would like it to be... In the case of desire it is, so to speak, the responsibility of the world to fit the content of the desire. [2004, pp. 167–68]

Though Searle indicates that desire takes the world to be "responsible" for conformity to its dictates, we all know that the world is, of course, responsible for no such thing. It is difficult to imagine what it would mean for the world itself to have responsibilities – and one wonders what could constitute a case of the world either meeting or shirking putative responsibilities. Facts need not conform to one's stubbornly fixed beliefs or desires.

The Inward Turn

Epictetus advised that our efforts should be directed only at "objects," or conditions, lying within our sphere of direct influence. Only those parts of the world (the "inner" world) that conform directly and without mediation to one's will are likely to conduce to the alleviation of distress and dissatisfaction – or what the Buddha regarded as dukkha. Again, Epictetus made this distinction between "internals" and "externals" a centerpiece of his counsel regarding the conduct of a well-regulated, rational lifestyle:

Remember that desire demands the attainment of that of which you are desirous; and aversion demands the avoidance of that to which you are averse; that he who fails of the object of his desires is disappointed; and he who incurs the object of his aversion is wretched. [*Enchiridion*, 2]

This is a central purpose of the Stoic's practice of self-discipline:

So, in our own case, we take it to be the work of one who

studies philosophy to bring his will into harmony with events; so that none of the things which happen may happen against our inclination, nor those which do not happen be desired by us. Hence they who have settled this point have it in their power never to be disappointed in what they seek, nor to incur what they shun; but to lead their own lives without sorrow, fear, or perturbation, and in society to preserve all the natural or acquired relations of son, father, brother, citizen, husband, wife, neighbor, fellow traveler, ruler, or subject. Something like this is what we take to be the work of a philosopher. [*Discourses*, p. 122]

It should be noted that bringing one's "will into harmony with events" does not imply a reflexive fatalism or simple-minded acquiescence irrespective of circumstances, but rather a recognition that many states of affairs are not, as Epictetus would put it, "up to us." One should not, for example, simply shrug at the criminal or refrain from attempting to reform him (if this appears possible). It may well be advisable, in fact, to imprison him (if he seems incorrigible). One should, however, recognize that criminality might (and probably will) persist irrespective of one's best efforts to dissuade criminals or counsel their rehabilitation. It is folly to peg one's contentment to another person's behavior or to defer equanimity until such time as all persons and conditions conform to one's stubbornly-held conceptions of how things "ought to be." The wise (or the skillful) understand the distinction between those conditions that lie within their control and those conditions that do not. It is selfish (or self-centered) desire that attempts to impose its dictates upon those phenomena over which it ultimately has no control. The self – or what one conceives of as the self – makes demands upon the "external" world, or upon "things which are beyond our power," as Epictetus puts it. This is the hallmark of selfish, or irrational and unskillful, desire. The "I" insists upon having its way – "The world must obey me!" Healthy (or skillful) desire, on the other hand, seeks to alter "internal" states that are "within our power," such as aversion, craving, attitude, etc. Skillful desire impels one to set about producing "inner" conformity with unalterable "external" conditions. This type of desire is adaptive to changing and uncontrollable conditions of reality.

Selfish desire seeks to impose itself upon other persons and states of affairs in the world "out there." When combined with the urge to eradicate those who disagree with one's worldview, this tends to generate needless conflict and suffering ensues. One may, of course, attempt to enlighten other persons, teaching them methods whereby they may attain serenity or equanimity, thereby attempting to "make the world a better place," but whether others heed that counsel is beyond the teacher's control. It is worth noting that wise men such as the Buddha and Epictetus were, after all, sometimes ignored and even ridiculed. Instead, we must embrace the world, its people, and its conditions by skillfully relinquishing the insistence that they must change in one way or another, and by employing rationally directed desire as a means of generating equanimity irrespective of the vicissitudes of our experience.

One need not renounce the desire to accept, embrace, or desist in one's opposition to conditions that lie beyond one's control. One need not renounce the desire for "self"-improvement and "self"-control, or even the desire to attempt to teach others how to improve themselves. Such desires, properly managed, may be very useful tools in the effort to reduce needless suffering. Epictetus and the Buddha do not proffer identical conceptions of the nature of the "self," but this does not preclude a deep confluence of practical counsel regarding the proper governance of desire and its relationship to living a wise and tranquil life.

Conclusion

Ancient Rome produced a sagacious counselor steeped in the

Western milieu, and Epictetus' wisdom survives and inspires even up to the present day, though the source of that wisdom is woefully under-appreciated and infrequently acknowledged. Epictetus' analysis of the distinction between "internals" and "externals" provides one useful way for Westerners to conceive Buddhist skillfulness with respect to desire and its possible concomitants. Epictetan counsel undoubtedly departs from the Buddha's worldview in certain respects (e.g. Stoic pantheism), but we should not, therefore, dismiss it as entirely alien to, or incompatible with, the Dhamma. Indeed, differences in manifestation are to be expected when the same truths are approached from disparate socio-cultural and historical starting points. Let us be prepared to explore, investigate, and respect wise counsel wherever we may find it – irrespective of cultural, geographical, or historical origin. Let us embrace all that is to be valued within our own heritage, but also reach out to find points of contact upon which further and richer understanding may develop between spiritual pilgrims from all points of the compass, thereby providing for mutual enrichment of their respective traditions and practices. We may find connections uniting us at greater depths than we had previously fathomed.

Chigurh's Coin: Karma and Chance in *No Country for Old Men*

Anton Chigurh kills people – but not always. Sometimes, he flips a coin. To all appearances, his would-be prey may be saved by correctly calling either heads or tails. There may be salvation, it seems, in the simplest game of chance. Heads you live, tails you die. So, does Chigurh actually dispense death at random? Not quite, and not usually – he has his reasons. On occasion, however, he offers the possible reprieve of the coin toss because, as he tells one of his victims, "That's the best that I can do." Chigurh is the irresistible force pervading every scene of *No Country for Old Men* (Coen Brothers, 2007). Even when he is not on camera, the viewer feels the weight of his presence and sees the toll it exacts upon every other significant character in the film. Even those who are fortunate enough to avoid actually meeting Chigurh find that they are altered, deeply disturbed, just knowing that such a man exists – and contemplating how and why such a man *can* exist. One aging lawman, having witnessed part of Chigurh's wake of destruction, declares, "It's just beyond everything!" We wish it were so, but Chigurh suggests that there may be no upper limit to human malefaction. This villain is not subject to our usual norms and expectations – even insofar as they pertain to villains and villainy.

There's Something About Chigurh

None of us knows quite what to make of Chigurh. His victims do not understand him, law enforcement officials are baffled by his exploits, the viewer is stunned by his ruthlessness, and yet there remains something about this figure that we cannot quite condemn. Is he, perhaps, *beyond* condemnation? Is there something, somehow, to *admire* in this man – even if it is only grudgingly and only at a safe distance that one may experience (or admit) this admiration? Perhaps Chigurh is intended to remain a bit of a cipher – an enigma. Even his name, after all, is awkward to both spell and pronounce. He eludes us. We are told of no childhood trauma, no biochemical imbalance or neurological impairment, no ancient outrage for which he now exacts revenge against society at large. We have no idea how he came to be this way – or even how one *can* become what we behold. There is money involved in the plot, but it becomes clear that this is not his primary motivation, nor is it a *sine qua non* of the film's evolution. The matter at issue could just as easily have been a package of cashews, a woman, or even an offhand remark (each of which plays its own cinematically ambiguous role in the encounters to be explored later). Chigurh kills almost as does a force of nature (albeit a selective one). Ahab was driven by his irrational hatred of the white whale. Chigurh, on the other hand, does not seem to be *driven* – he just seems to *be*. Chigurh kills. That is what he does. So... why toss the coin?

Picture the following scene. A man, known to the viewer to be a ruthless murderer, dripping with obvious menace, flips a coin, and demands that his helpless prey, "Call it." In such a scenario, is the murder (or lack thereof) causally determined by the flip of the coin (as opposed to something deep within the killer's psyche)? What if the victim makes the wrong call or, more interestingly, refuses to make any call on the grounds that the "game" is disingenuous, degrading, or perverse? How do we assess the culpability of the killer? He is, of course, the one pulling the trigger – but antecedent events (though inaccessible to the viewer) have undoubtedly contributed to his character, and to current contingencies. Does the killer "have to" kill? Is he compelled by his nature, his history, or (perhaps) his "principles" (perverse though they may be)? Are his victims constrained to lay themselves in his path, or could events have turned out differently? All of these questions, and several corollaries flow as an undercurrent through the recent Oscar-winning

Coen Brothers film. These questions are not quite answered, however, and the viewer is left, if that viewer is attentive, with an interesting set of issues to ponder regarding the nature of the psychopath Anton Chigurh (including the question of whether he *is*, in fact, properly characterized as a psychopath). He appears to operate in accordance with something like an "ethical code" (though, again, the term is severely deformed in this context). Can we decipher his code? Should we *want* to do so, or are some matters better left beyond our understanding? Then there is the matter of assessing the victims and their behavior. Are any of them properly regarded as morally responsible for the persons that they become and/or the manner in which their lives unfold? As one of them tells his wife, early in the film, "Baby, things happen."

I wish to consider three distinct, but not entirely separable, encounters between the lethally cold-blooded Anton Chigurh, and three relatively peripheral characters whose misfortune (or is it, perhaps, something closer to karma?) places them at the mercy of the killer's whim – and, in two of the three cases, apparently also at the mercy of a tossed coin. The first incident leads the viewer to believe that properly calling the coin toss can save the potential victim, as doing so appears actually to salvage the life of a hapless gas station owner. It is, however, noted by the final not-so-lucky victim that the coin, in and of itself, does not determine the death or survival of those who cross Chigurh's path. The coin, as she puts it, "don't have no say." It is, after all, merely a coin, an inert object, and not an agent. Chigurh, it would seem, can pull the trigger irrespective of the coin coming up either heads or tails. He does not, in fact, even have to toss the coin – yet something more is at work here. Blame is not so easily affixed as surface events would indicate. As Chigurh himself tells his final victim in the film (but not, the viewer suspects, his final victim altogether), "I got here the same way the coin did." He and the coin are both travelers, storm tossed perhaps, to this place, this time, and, it would appear, this brutal dispensation. Chigurh is, as are the rest of us, at least in significant respects, a product of heredity and environment, nature and nurture (or, perhaps in Chigurh's case, a lack of the latter). Let us consider the three instances in which Chigurh's words and actions seem to suggest an ambiguous interplay of both fortune and determinism, in the form of complexly interwoven karmic consequences of actions performed (or omitted) by various characters in the film. Doing so may be the key to grasping the tale's significance – the meaning (if there is one) behind the grizzly events within this disturbing but brilliant character study of an enigmatic angel of death and the persistent failure of both his victims and law enforcement officials to (if the pun may be pardoned) make heads or tails of the man.

The Price of Gas

In the first case, an unnamed gas station owner/attendant encounters Chigurh and makes a seemingly innocuous remark that nonetheless trips some switch in the villain's psyche. As their exchange begins to take on an edgy intensity, it becomes clear to the viewer, as well as to the stunned and helpless old man, that Chigurh is contemplating a deployment of his craft. He is clearly considering a murder. Chigurh's demeanor alone makes this obvious – even to a complete stranger. He has the ability to become malignity incarnate within the blink of an eye. At the apex of the intensity, Chigurh asks, "What is the most that you have ever lost on a coin toss?" Before the stunned old man can stammer out a complete answer, Chigurh flips a coin, covers it with his hand, and demands, "Call it... Friendo." His tone is belligerent and threatening, but also acutely controlled. There is no doubt about which party is master of the station owner's fate.

When the old man hesitantly protests that he hasn't "put nothin' up," Chigurh icily insists that, indeed, he has been "putting it up" his whole life. Chigurh seems especially perturbed by the fact that the old man has, as he puts it, "married into it" (i.e. that he has come to his current position willfully and, perhaps, without earning his station). There seems to be an implication, at least as far as Chigurh is concerned, that the old man's actions have brought this moment into being. Still stunned, and clearly terrified, the man asks what he stands to win, and Chigurh coolly replies, "Everything... now call it." Both understand what is on the line, but only one seems to have any inkling as to why it should be so. Luckily for the old man, he calls the coin's fall correctly, and Chigurh allows him to keep the quarter (not to mention his life – he has, quite literally, been "given quarter") as a souvenir of their encounter. As the man moves to put it in his pocket, however, Chigurh admonishes him not to do so, because then it will mix with his other change, and he will cease to identify it as his *lucky* quarter. It would become like any other coin in his pocket and, as Chigurh points out, that is precisely what it is – but it is also the quarter that saved his life (or, at least, caused Chigurh not to *take* his life).

So, did properly calling the coin toss actually save this would-be murder victim? Did Chigurh simply grant him clemency or experience some spontaneous abatement of the killer's urge? Is it, somehow, both luck and psychosis that explain the outcome of this bizarre encounter? It would appear that a random (or, at least, unpredictable) event, the coin toss, played a causally determinative role within the context of the film's unfolding. The viewer is left with the clear impression that an incorrect call, or no call at all, would have resulted in yet another murder (by this point in the film, Chigurh has already killed with even less provocation). This suspicion seems to be confirmed by the third encounter we shall consider. It involves an equally helpless but, somehow, more dignified character – one that seems to have caught an intuitive glimpse of the full depth and darkness of Chigurh's involutedly unique psyche.

All's Well that Ends Wells

Our second incident involves something of an apparently more personal nature, and a victim for whom the viewer experiences somewhat less sympathy. This time Chigurh has the drop on the overly self-assured bounty hunter, Carson Wells. Furthermore, Chigurh seems to have developed a degree of genuine personal distaste for this man, and the viewer finds it difficult not to agree with this appraisal. Wells is something of an arrogant, predatory, manipulative jackal himself. He makes his living by scavenging the remains of ruined lives and by hunting (and, we are led to believe, sometimes killing) men that, we cannot help but suspect, are not quite so different from Wells himself. In an earlier conversation Wells almost admits as much. In this instance, however, his arrogance proves to be his undoing. In this instance, he is overmatched. Chigurh is manifestly not, as Wells had earlier assured his employer, a "garden variety homicidal maniac." Chigurh seems to be affronted by the fact that Wells does not recognize that he is up against a higher order of being than his typical quarry. This time, there is no offer of a coin flip. The bounty hunter will not be granted the possibility of reprieve, or even the illusion of such a possibility. It is made clear to him that his time is at an end. Chigurh even points out that it would be more dignified for Wells to admit that he is doomed, and asks, "If the rule that you have followed has brought you to this point... then of what use is the rule?" When he begins asking the question, he is smiling – by the time he concludes, he is not. In desperation, Wells offers Chigurh a large sum of cash as ransom in exchange for his life and says, not very convincingly, "You don't have to do this." Chigurh, with a contemptuous half-smile replies, "They all say that," and, at a cinematically opportune moment, fires his shotgun (equipped with a silencer) into the bounty hunter's torso. Chigurh's emotional response to the event is less pronounced than the typical man's concern at having swatted a mosquito. He answers a ringing phone and props his feet on the bed so that his shoes will not become soaked with Wells' blood as it slowly spills out and covers the floor of the hotel room. Unfortunately for his interlocutor in our third scenario, the call is from Llewelyn Moss – and their conversation does not suit Chigurh's sense of (shall we say) "justice."

The Coin Don't Have No Say

In the final of the three encounters presented here, the somewhat dim, but nonetheless intuitive Carla Jean Moss, wife of the aforementioned Llewelyn Moss, ends up where we suspected all along that she might. Her husband set much of the film's chain reaction of carnage in motion by helping himself to two million dollars that Chigurh regards as rightfully (if that term is permissible here) his. Mrs. Moss finds herself seated across from the emotionless Chigurh, who has just recently killed Llewelyn (not to mention a few other unlucky peripheral folk who happened to be in the vicinity of his target). Interestingly, Chigurh, during their phone conversation, had promised Llewelyn that he would allow Carla Jean to live if the money with which Llewelyn had absconded were to be returned to Chigurh (and, it is worth noting, *laid at his feet*). He assures Llewelyn that that is the best deal he has to offer. It is "the best he can do." Llewelyn is to die in either case (it seems a matter of "principle"), but his wife, Chigurh promises (sincerely, we suspect), can be spared if his orders are obeyed. Llewelyn is, alas, not the obedient sort and, after dispensing with the outmanned husband in his preferred fashion, Chigurh pays a visit to Carla Jean – as if duty-bound by his threat to do so. He tells Carla Jean that Llewelyn could have saved her but stubbornly chose not to accept the conditions for her survival. Carla Jean declares both her ignorance of her husband's plan and her general innocence in this matter. She tells Chigurh, as he has previously noted that "they" all do, "You don't have to do this." After a moment's hesitation, which is significant insofar as the viewer has been given the impression that this is a man who does not often hesitate, Chigurh offers her the same coin flip reprieve he had previously offered the lucky old man at the gas station. With a defiance that is, on the one hand, simple-minded, but also, somehow, a noble refusal to indulge in Chigurh's game, Carla Jean refuses to "call it" when prompted to do so after the coin has been flipped and covered by Chigurh's hand. She refuses on the grounds that, as she puts it, "The coin don't have no say in it – it's just you." Chigurh, with an expression indicating something between exasperation (the type one might express toward a dimwitted but lovely child) and a resigned indifference (almost), points out that he "got here the same way as the coin did." Again, there is the intimation that the business of life and death is not entirely up to him – and not quite so fascinating to him as to everyone else. This is simply what he does. We sense that there are rules to this game that only the killer understands.

A few moments later, we see Chigurh checking the soles of his shoes outside the house in which, we are left to assume, Carla Jean's blood now covers some significant portion of the floor. Was Carla Jean correct? Is the coin simply a prop in a pointlessly cruel and manipulative game? Was it really an act of courage to refuse to participate in a ludicrous and macabre pretense – or did she stubbornly waste her one chance at survival (as her husband, and his foolish pride, had let a prior chance slip away)? The viewer is left with the impression that there is some sense in which, unlike her husband and Carson Wells, Carla Jean did not "have to" die. Would Chigurh (*could* Chigurh) have allowed her to live if she had simply made the lucky call – much as he had permitted the old man at the gas station to continue drawing breath? We, and she, will never know. The role of the coin remains ambiguous.

Compared to What?

To what extent, and in what sense, can Chigurh's actions

(not to mention the actions of the other characters) in the aforementioned incidents be legitimately described as "free"? Does the coin-flipping ritual actually determine this murderer's next move – in those cases in which the flip is even on offer? Is it really up to Chigurh, ultimately, that he tenders some potential victims the possibility of reprieve (or, at least, the appearance of such a possibility), or is his pathology, in conjunction with antecedent events, the real determinant of life-and-death in these cases? Perhaps Chigurh is just a killing machine with a built-in abort system that may be triggered under fortuitous circumstances. *No Country for Old Men* seems to offer a portrait of a man with robust, though imperfect, control over external events and persons that he encounters, but leaves an ambiguous accounting of that same man's control over his own internal drives and actions. He grants clemency when the call properly coincides with the toss of the coin, but it is, of course, *he* who tosses the coin – or does not. He seems uninterested in questions of moral right and wrong (as commonly understood), but keenly attuned to matters of simple (or not-so-simple) cause and effect, as well as violations of his "ethical code." As far as Chigurh is concerned, his victims cause their own demise (or secure their survival) through their behaviors. He seems, at some points in the narrative, to behave as an instrument of karmic consequence; he ensures that others reap what, in his estimation, they have sown. We see the outwardly observable expressions of his inner drives issuing in massacre as he carves a swath through those who keep telling him, "You don't have to do this." His responses and mannerisms imply that he *does* have to "do this," because it is either his nature, or it is the product of some irrevocable commitment that leaves him, quite unrepentantly, determined to "do this." He almost seems to want to say, "Don't you people see that this is just what I do? I kill." Indeed, the arrogant Carson Wells almost suggests as much when, in answer to a question about how dangerous Chigurh really is, he replies,

"Compared to what... bubonic plague?" Unfortunately for Wells, he underestimates the uniquely lethal ruthlessness and ingenuity of this particular adversary. He assumes that Chigurh is just a particularly clever lunatic out on a killing spree. The viewer knows better. Chigurh is something closer to a force of nature – as inexorable and disinterested in human life as a flood, earthquake, or, indeed, a plague. Carla Jean, Llewelyn, Carson Wells, and many other denizens of the country that is no place for old men, find this out the hard way.

Hard Bark

In the film's final scene, Sheriff Bell tells his wife of a dream he has lately had. Bell has kept tabs on Chigurh's exploits and has seen the rivers of blood produced in the wake of Chigurh's progress, but he has failed (just barely) to catch up with this man who lays waste to nearly everyone and everything in his path. As a result, at least in part, of Chigurh's exploits, Bell has decided to quit his job as sheriff because, as he tells his brother (who has been shot and partially paralyzed by another criminal), "I feel overmatched." Bell has met up with something that he does not understand. The film opened with Bell's voice-over and his expression of stunned disjointedness as he observes a new form of criminality that seems recalcitrant and unmotivated – resistant to any taxonomy within Bell's experience or imagination. There is a new darkness afoot, and Bell cannot get his mind around it.

In the dream as he describes it to his wife, Bell's father, another lawman, long since dead, rides into a dark wilderness carrying fire, and the sheriff knows (somehow) that his dad is waiting for him. The filmmakers leave us (or, at least, leave me) with the impression that Mr. Chigurh may have a hand in reuniting Bell and his late father. Chigurh knows that Bell has been on his trail and, as Wells has pointed out, Chigurh objects to such "inconveniences" as having to evade officers of the law for which he exhibits nothing but contempt and disregard – and the viewer knows what Chigurh did to the first cop that he met in the film.

One suspects that no coin toss will postpone the reunion of Bell and his deceased father. It is difficult to imagine the taciturn (former) Sheriff Bell submitting to Chigurh's game, and Chigurh seems to be an acutely adept judge of character, so we suspect that he will forgo the offer. In Bell's case, it would constitute an insult – and it is not as if Chigurh holds any personal grudge against the man. He is simply an "inconvenience" to be dealt with in the most expedient fashion. Bell appears to understand, better than any other character in the film (with the notable exception of Chigurh himself), that encounters with this predator are determined by inexorable forces that pay no heed to any exigencies of the human condition. Chigurh is something more than a merchant of death, something more implacable than "the ultimate badass," as was earlier suggested by the stubborn and ill-fated Llewelyn Moss. Chigurh is the inevitable. He is the embodiment of the darkness that Bell cannot understand. The thing about the inevitable is that there just is no getting around it. Chigurh will not relent. As Bell puts it in his typical understated fashion, "He's got some hard bark on him."

Call It

Randomness, fate, karma, moral right and wrong, and all related considerations are, perhaps, beside the point (at least insofar as the film is concerned). Bell's wilderness awaits us all. Those who encounter Chigurh just tend to get there a bit sooner than they might otherwise have expected. That is simply what Chigurh does. That is simply what he is. His role, as he conceives it, is fairly well defined. When his victims plead, "You don't have to do this," they misconstrue his nature – and he regards this as laughable, perhaps even a pathetic form of naïveté or willful ignorance. Chigurh is what the world has made him. He pulls the trigger, but his victims keep placing themselves in his crosshairs. They have all been "putting it up" their whole lives. Chigurh is the implement linking karma and consequence – as he is also a product of karma and consequence. Killing machines do not simply fall from the sky. They are, somehow or other, *made* – and the wheel of life and death goes round and round. Occasionally, a coin is tossed.

Is Chigurh responsible for his character, for his horrifying deeds, for the monster that he has become? What of the other characters in the film? Why have they been drawn into Chigurh's sphere of influence – his deadly gravitational pull? Llewelyn Moss took some money that did not belong to him. Of course, he also did not know that it "belonged" to Chigurh. Carla Jean simply had the misfortune of being married to Llewelyn. Then again, she *did* marry him. Carson Wells had the temerity to try to kill or capture (we suspect he preferred to kill) Chigurh. The man is, however, a bounty hunter, and was offered a lot of money to ply his trade. Many other characters just happened to be driving down the wrong road at the wrong time, sitting behind the wrong desk, or drinking beer beside the wrong hotel pool. Even in these instances, however, we might ask what led them to that particular place and time. In fact, and this may be the real point, we may ask what leads *any of us* to this place, this time, this character, these proclivities, this life unfolding all around and through us. Are any of us, ultimately, authors of the selves into which we evolve? Are any of us in control of the twists and turns our lives take – or are we all simply caught in the turning, grinding wheel of karma (or fate, or destiny, or randomness, or call-it-what-you-like)? What are we to make of Anton Chigurh? Well, he is someone with whom we do not wish to make acquaintance. That much is clear. Beyond that, answers and explanations are elusive. Perhaps there is a more crucial and more immediate question, and perhaps we will ask it if we are attentive to this extraordinary film – and if we have the intestinal fortitude to sift honestly through the stuff of our lives and character. The question is this: What are we to make of *ourselves*? How far (and by what exactly) are we removed from, different from, the likes of Anton Chigurh? Call it... Friendo.

Eternal Selves and The Problem of Evil

You cannot begin to understand suffering from this side of eternity.
– Kimber Kauffman

Some claim that only the intellectually defective can fail to be impressed by the inconsistency between belief in the existence of the theistic God and the recognition of suffering in our world – especially given the quantity and intensity of human suffering. An omniscient, omnipotent, omni-benevolent God would not allow his beloved children to suffer, and certainly not as often or as intensely as they do. A good God would not permit evils to relentlessly afflict human life within His creation. The ubiquity of suffering renders belief in the perfect God of theism irrational. So say anti-theistic proponents of the problem of evil.

Theists, however, may have an insufficiently appreciated response to this line of attack. If theists can avail themselves of the identification of persons with eternal beings (as opposed to mere mortal bodies), then human suffering is more readily reconcilable with the existence of a good God. Identifying persons with eternal souls (or transcendent selves) insulates the theist from the traditional problem of evil by providing a counterweight against the disturbing vicissitudes of embodied existence (though the insulation is, of course, purchased only at the expense of defending the plausibility of postmortem personal survival – no small task). The actual existence of eternal selves is, obviously, a contentious issue and is worthy (or unworthy) of debate on its own merits. Theologians, biblical exegetes and others will likely never tire of debating the proper interpretation of scriptural passages regarding the existence and nature of the soul, the afterlife, etc. I do not, however, need to defend the immateriality or eternality of the soul (or the persistence of a postmortem self) in this paper. My point is merely that a theist

112

who can make the case for a Platonic, Augustinian, Cartesian, or otherwise transcendent account of the "true self" has, thereby, a potentially potent response to the traditional problem of evil. If persons are properly identified with something like disembodied (or resurrected) eternal selves that transcend the material world, then the apparently gratuitous suffering of the better part of humanity may be neatly reconciled with the existence of the theistic God. If our suffering is merely apparent, or afflicts only a minuscule portion of our total existence, then theism (on this score, at least) may be salvageable.

It is not clear that nonphysical entities *can* suffer as a result of bodily damage and our variegated encounters with the natural world. Even if immaterial selves can somehow suffer along with the physical body, it seems that an embodied lifetime of suffering must shrink to insignificance by comparison with a postmortem eternity free of all physical frailties. Theists can argue that an obsessive and myopic concern with bodily suffering motivates the problem of evil, and that this obsession is the result of an unenlightened attachment to an ephemeral physical realm. They can, that is, if the case can be made for the eternal postmortem persistence of persons (or selves). If our bodies are not quite ourselves after all, and if the true self is eternal, then comparatively little (if any) evil befalls the beloved children of God in this brief embodied existence (appearances to the contrary notwithstanding).

The Problem of Evil

Theism is plagued with the problem of evil. Not only within philosophical circles, but also among the general public, the most common and persistent challenge to the existence of an all-good, all-powerful, and all-knowing deity is the complaint that human life is saturated with pain and suffering. Everyone suffers to some degree. Some, even apparent innocents, suffer hideous torment and die in ways that many regard as heartbreaking and irremediably evil. Just consider man's hideous inhumanity to man in the form of phenomena such as slavery or the horrors of warfare and state-sponsored holocaust. Further consider the suffering resulting from natural disasters and plagues that sweep indiscriminately through defenseless populations. Anyone that watches television news broadcasts or reads a newspaper will be confronted with relentless daily images and accounts of disease, famine, oppression, murder, rape, child molestation, and other natural and man-made horrors. The litany of human suffering could continue literally *ad nauseum*. The world is a fearful place, and no one gets out alive. How could a good God allow this?

The problem of evil, as it is typically presented, is really the problem of suffering (particularly *human* suffering). How, we are asked, can an omniscient, omnipotent, omni-benevolent God allow needless and gratuitous suffering in the form of moral evil (e.g. murder, rape, child molestation, warfare, etc.), and/or natural evil (e.g. famine, pestilence, natural disasters, etc.) to befall innocent persons – especially in ways that do not appear to generate commensurate or countervailing goods? Surely, it is argued, a good God with the power and foreknowledge to prevent such suffering would have done so. Clearly, suffering does occur – in fact, a clearly gratuitous quantity of it occurs. In the face of incontrovertible evidence of worldly imperfection, continued belief in the perfect God of theism is, according to proponents of the problem of evil, indefensible. The following is a fairly standard formulation of the argument that the existence of an omniscient, omnipotent, omni-benevolent God (the "3-O" God for short) is incompatible with the world as we experience it:

1. If God is omniscient, then God knows when, where, and how human suffering will occur if it is not prevented.
2. If God is omnipotent, then God has the power to prevent each instance of human suffering.

3. If God is omni-benevolent, then God wants to prevent each instance of human suffering.

4. So, if there exists a God who knows how to prevent human suffering, has the power to prevent it, and wants to prevent it (i.e. if the "3-O" God exists), then human suffering will not occur.

5. Human suffering occurs (relentlessly and ubiquitously).

C. Therefore, the "3-O" God does not exist – and theism is false.

Perhaps there is no deity at all, or perhaps there is a god whose power, or knowledge, or virtue is less than perfect. But clearly the perfect God of theism cannot have allowed the world to come to this sorry state – or so it seems to those who claim that the problem of evil confutes theism.

Theodicies

Theists have constructed a variety of theodicies (i.e. attempts to reconcile the presence of suffering in our world with the existence of a "3-O" God) in response to the problem of evil. These typically attack premise three in the above argument. The free will defense contends that evil is due to the immoral actions of free agents, but that the world is better with free, morally responsible persons in it than with automata who lack moral responsibility altogether. The greater good's defense asserts that evils are necessary for the existence of greater or "second-order" goods such as courage, forgiveness, sympathy, moral urgency, etc., and that the world is better with these greater goods (and the evils that they necessitate) than without them. Irenaean-style "soul-making" theodicies combine the free will and greater good defenses insofar as humankind is portrayed as imperfect and unfinished, and it is asserted that God offers a hedonically challenging reality so that people can freely choose to improve their souls within a world that provides obstructions, pitfalls, dangers, temptations and so on. In one way or another, all these theodicies suggest that an omni-benevolent God need not oppose the existence of any and all causes of human suffering. Instead, it is suggested that a perfectly good God will create the best of all possible worlds, and that this best of all possible worlds necessarily involves the existence of various types of evil as ineliminable prerequisites or consequences of higher or countervailing goods (e.g. free will, opportunities for self-perfection, experience of moral urgency, etc.). These goods warrant the evils that they necessitate. Hence, upon careful analysis, we find that there is no inconsistency between the existence of the "3-O" God and the presence of human suffering because human suffering serves a central purpose in the best of all possible worlds. So say the theodicists.

Suffering and A Good God

Proponents of the problem of evil are seldom persuaded by these efforts at reconciliation, as they claim that the theistic God could have obviated suffering altogether in our world or, at the very least, could have prevented much of our suffering without commensurate loss of goods. Surely, the best of all possible worlds ought to contain far less suffering than does the actual world. The quantity and intensity of actual human suffering is clearly gratuitous and unwarranted by the allegedly countervailing goods. No theodicy, they claim, can salvage theism in the face of the world as we experience it.

The pseudonymous BC Johnson, for example, argues that all of the aforementioned theodicies are inadequate and/or fallacious. None, he claims, consistently retains God's omnipotence, omniscience, and omni-benevolence in their attempted justifications of human pain and suffering. He concludes:

The various excuses theists offer for why God has allowed evil to exist have been demonstrated to be inadequate. However, the conclusive objection to these excuses does not depend on their inadequacy... Every excuse we could provide to make the world consistent with a good God can be paralleled by an excuse to make the world consistent with an evil God. This is so because the world is a mixture of both good and bad. [1981, pp. 106–7]

One cannot, Johnson suggests, reconcile an observably imperfect world with belief in a perfect creator of that world. The various theodicies are vain and *ad hoc* attempts to attribute apparent goodness to God's will while systematically refusing to acknowledge that the same arguments can be stood on their head and presented as justification for imputing evil to God's will on the basis of the very same observable phenomena.

Even theists are sometimes hard-pressed to find a justification for the horrific suffering in (what they claim to be) God's creation. Emil Fackenheim, a survivor of Auschwitz, despairs of rationally reconciling the theistic God with the abomination of the concentration camps:

... [T]he search for a purpose in Auschwitz is foredoomed to total failure. Not that good men in their despair have not made the attempt. Good Orthodox Jews have resorted to the ancient "for our sins we are punished," but this recourse, unacceptable already to Job, is in this case all the more impossible. A good Christian theologian sees the purpose of Auschwitz as a divine reminder of the sufferings of Christ, but this testifies to a moving sense of desperation – and to an incredible lapse of theological judgment. A good Jewish secularist will connect the Holocaust with the rise of the state of Israel, but while to see a causal connection here is possible and necessary, to see a purpose is intolerable. A total and uncompromising sweep must be made of these and other explanations, all designed to give purpose to Auschwitz. No purpose, religious or non-religious, will ever be found in Auschwitz. The very attempt to find one is blasphemous. [1978, p. 29]

To many, it seems that the immensity of human suffering resists reconciliation with the existence of an all-powerful and loving God. Theists, however, can argue that the apparent incompatibility arises from a misguided conception of human suffering and personhood. Critics of theism may be correct in their assertion that the "3-O" God's existence is inconsistent with human suffering as it is typically characterized. If, however, the typical focus on embodied suffering is misleading or inapt, then the apparent inconsistency may be resolved.

All of the aforementioned theodicies, objections against them and subsequent replies seem to take for granted the thesis that persons truly suffer, and most take for granted an apparent excess of suffering that, at the very least, requires special explanation. Theodicists seldom challenge premise five in the aforementioned formulation of the problem of evil – and this may be an oversight. That humans suffer a great deal may seem about as obvious and uncontroversial a claim as any philosopher could hope to encounter, but it may be inadvisable for theists to blithely accept this supposition. The theist can argue that, ultimately, the "evils" that befall us may do our true selves less damage than our embodied selves perceive. In fact, it may well be that suffering is, as has been suggested by various philosophers and religious figures, illusory. It is possible that *our true selves* do not suffer at all.

Even if our suffering turns out to be quite real, it is not clear why the theist should find this especially troubling – so long as that theist is also committed to the eternality of the true self. If persons are correctly identified with eternal souls (or imperishable selves), then our concern with human suffering must be altered in light of considerations surrounding the postmortem persistence of persons.

Eternal Selves

If persons are not, as many have suggested, properly identifiable with physical bodies, but rather with (something like) immaterial and/or eternal souls, then it is not at all clear that persons are susceptible of suffering as a result of natural evils or the moral misdeeds of others. Even if injury does somehow penetrate through to the soul or the immaterial self, the totality of embodied suffering would seem to be dwarfed by comparison with an eternity of postmortem experience. Let us first consider just the potential immateriality of the self, apart from considerations relating to eternality.

Immaterial selves cannot be murdered, raped, molested, or otherwise damaged by physical villainy, nor can they be broken, burned, infected, or otherwise injured by the body's encounters with the natural world. An immaterial being would appear to be well insulated from the kinds of troubles that befall material bodies. Fackenheim tells us that, "Eichmann sought to destroy both bodies and souls" [p. 27], but it is not clear how Eichmann could have literally succeeded in the latter project so long as selves are ultimately immaterial entities. If persons are properly identifiable with immaterial beings, then upon bodily death (and, presumably, liberation from the susceptibilities of embodiment), persons will undergo something akin to awakening from a dream (or perhaps a nightmare) to find that their terrestrial experiences have been not quite veridical (or, perhaps, not quite completely understood). Though interpretations of scriptural mention of the nature of the soul and afterlife are contentious, Matthew 10:28 advises us:

Do not be afraid of those who kill the body but cannot kill the soul. Rather, be afraid of the One who can destroy both soul and body in hell. [emphasis added]

Perhaps God can destroy the immaterial soul, but it is not at all clear how a mere man (such as Eichmann) or the physical power of natural forces can do so. The efficacy of the torturer's instruments seems limited to the physical realm. It is suggested that we, therefore, have no reason to fear despoilers of the body. They cannot harm the true self – or, perhaps, can do it comparatively negligible harm.

Suppose, however, that this is mistaken. Suppose that the victim's soul is a material entity and does somehow suffer along with the victim's body (or that immaterial entities can – somehow – suffer damage resulting from association with physical bodies). Let us imagine a life like Job's, but absent the restoration to relative happiness after his encounter with the whirlwind. Let us imagine, in fact, the most hedonically challenged life in human history, complete with the maximum possible dispersal of suffering to the soul (whatever that would mean exactly) over the course of this unfortunate person's embodied life. If the true self is eternal, then any impingements upon it during the person's embodied lifetime can amount to no more than a vanishingly minute portion of that self's experience over the course of its eternal existence. The most hideous embodied life that we can imagine is tantamount to no more than a pinprick by comparison with a postmortem eternity. No matter the severity or intensity of one's terrestrial suffering, one's subsequent eternal experience must, of mathematical necessity, dwarf the dissatisfaction accumulated from cradle to grave. Intense, ceaseless suffering throughout a full, torturous lifetime would seem, nonetheless, to be bounded by bodily death. Even if injury is transmitted to the soul or the true self and leaves indelible scarring there, an eternal postmortem existence provides infinite time to heal all wounds. Since the total accumulation of wounds is finite, an eternity free of them should more than suffice as a palliative. Or so it would seem.

Time Heals All Wounds

Let us imagine that someone recently departed from a miserable terrestrial existence encounters God (however that is best understood) and, in an accusatory tone, instigates the following exchange with the Almighty:

> Postmortem Person: Why did you allow me to suffer so much throughout my whole life? I did nothing to deserve so much suffering, and I demand an explanation!
>
> God: I will explain after you have spent 100 billion earth years free from the tribulations that you knew in the body. In the meantime, remember that your life has not ended – in many ways it has really just begun.

While this hypothetical exchange is, admittedly, a bit of a caricature, we can nonetheless suspect that this sort of complaint must diminish over the eons. Whatever the character of the afterlife, must not the eternal experience thereof dwarf the entirety of one's earthly sorrows – however great they may have seemed during the embodied lifetime? Perhaps this is why John Hick says:

> As we saw when discussing the problem of evil, *no theodicy can succeed without drawing into itself this eschatological faith in an eternal, and therefore infinite, good which thus outweighs all the pains and sorrows that have been endured on the way to it.* [1963, pp. 52–53 – emphasis added]

Surely, the view from eternity must provide something of a new perspective on the evaluation of life in the body. Eternity must trump a finite interval of suffering. It is, therefore, not obvious that human suffering is irreconcilable with theism.

Resistance Is Futile: Stoic Counsel About "Externals"

Axiom of Futility. Agents are required not to make direct attempts to do (or be) something that is logically, theoretically, or practically impossible.
– Becker [p. 42]

To be happy, we must not be too concerned with others.
– Albert Camus

Emotional and psychological attachment to futile endeavors assures frustration, anxiety, and discontent. Insisting that the external world must conform to one's stubbornly-held desires and preconceived expectations virtually guarantees dissatisfaction. Such insistence is futile. I contend that unhealthy attachments of this nature are an astoundingly common, but readily eradicable, source of needless distress.

> Perhaps no school of philosophy in the ancient world placed greater emphasis on the importance of understanding and accepting the limits of human power than did the Stoics. For the Stoics maintain that in addition to knowing what is worth doing, wisdom, in some very fundamental way, consists in knowing what is and is not in our power, and not attempting to do what we cannot do. [2001, p. 75]

In particular, I contend that all psychological dependence upon such Stoic "externals" as the behaviors and cognitive states of persons other than oneself are subsumable under the epigrammatic Stoic Axiom of Futility. In other words, we invite needless suffering when we tether our contentment to conditions, such as the beliefs, attitudes, and behaviors of others, that lie beyond our sphere of direct, practical control. Any attempt to govern another agent's beliefs, desires, or behavior constitutes a futile effort to control phenomena that are, in the language of Epictetus' *Enchiridion*, "not up to us." There is a sense in which this is a trivial and obvious observation – we cannot control other people, their thoughts, etc. Nearly everyone understands this, and few would openly dispute any such assertion. Nonetheless, the pervasive and seemingly incorrigible insistence upon attempting to do so, and the tendency to become distressed at the failure of such attempts, warrants careful analysis and cries out for therapeutic counsel. The effort to formulate and *offer* helpful counsel is *not* futile. Composing and communicating advice is, for all practical purposes, within my control (provided that brain and body do not fail me). Insisting upon the efficacy or acceptance of such counsel is, however, a quixotic and futile bit of stubbornness – destined to result in psychological and emotional distress. I can write this article defending and explaining a little valuable Stoic counsel as best I am able (and that effort is entirely "up to me"), but I am a fool if I allow my emotional well-being to depend upon the article being accepted at an academic conference, selected for publication, or upon anyone reading it, taking it seriously, or adhering to the counsel offered herein. The wise attitude regarding the acceptance of proffered counsel is rational detachment, and recognition that such matters are simply not within the counselor's control. That is the Stoic's advice – take it or leave it.

Futility and Discontent

Surely, some will contend, limiting our endeavors and concerns in this fashion is bound to stultify development and inhibit the kinds of hopes and dreams that have driven innovation, technological achievement, and nearly every form of advancement from which humanity has enjoyed benefit. We must dare, even in the face of futility, to risk failure. Only through such daring is real progress realized. Let us dare great deeds and, if we fail to achieve them, glory nonetheless in our valiant struggle and derive both pride and hope from "dreaming the impossible dream." Don Quixote may be a tragic hero, but he is a *hero* nonetheless, precisely because he "tilted at windmills" and enlarged his spirit thereby. The inspiration is worth braving defeat and humiliation. Our culture is, for good reason, saturated with expressions of admiration for those who dare, those who dream, those who persevere in the face of seemingly impossible obstacles and brutal travails. We Americans, after all, "Remember the Alamo!" The birth of the United States as a nation is inextricably dependent upon braving terrifying odds and summoning the courage to combat an ostensibly insurmountable challenge, an undefeatable adversary. Consider the stirrings conjured by a mention of Valley Forge. Who among us does not root for the underdog, and "hope against hope" when faced with a lost cause? Patron saints do not, after all, generally live lives of luxury, or die peaceful, gentle deaths. Does Stoicism counsel cowardice, acquiescence, and quietism? If so, then its counsel is ignoble at best, and is apt to diminish those who embrace it. Marvin Kohl nicely articulates this ancient complaint:

> Some thinkers may immediately object to this line of thinking and say that to be failure-proof one must have an unconquerable faith in being able to do anything one wants to do. Others may urge us to believe that invincible determination of purpose should be psychologically so fixed that we persevere until "either victory or death." Still others, operating under the pretense of wisdom, may urge us to combine a false with a true statement. Here we are told that "you can have anything you want, but you can't have it all." These extreme libertarians of choice reject the precept that one ought not try to do things that are known to be impossible or, and more important, that very few things

are, in fact, impossible. Like Nicholas Rescher, they are also inclined to believe as a general life stance that optimal results are attainable only by trying for too much. [2001, p. 78]

So goes a fairly standard objection against "lowering one's aim" in order that one may avoid disappointment. First of all, it is practically impossible that any endeavor may be *known* to be futile. We have all heard "stranger things have happened," offered as encouragement and exhortation. Secondly, even a truly futile endeavor may have an ennobling quality not otherwise attainable – an ennobling power that countervails the detriments of failure. We admire those who endure, those who strive, and those glorious "fools" willing to "fight the unbeatable foe." Such sentiments may be poetic – but poetry makes for lousy philosophy, and impractical counsel.

This objection is misguided on two fronts. As Kohl reminds us, the Stoics long ago argued that:

The point… is that to aim at what cannot be done is not only to invite failure but to waste precious time and energy that could have been effective elsewhere. To aim at the futile with indefeasible resolution and the profound conviction that one must persevere to "either victory or death" is to invite the latter and is, therefore, even more seriously normatively flawed. [2001, p. 78]

Every moment spent in pursuit of the impossible, the *futile*, is a moment lost to the effort to attain the attainable. Our time and our energy are limited. It is irrational and self-defeating to sacrifice a potential benefit in the futile attempt to gain the unattainable boon. This is the classic "sucker's bet." Furthermore, successful ventures are not, inherently, less ennobling than are quixotic quests. The Alamo would still be worth remembering had Santa Anna's legions faltered and turned back – perhaps even more so! Surely, failure is not a *necessary* condition for optimizing consequences over the long term, nor is it necessary for sublime experience. Were it so, we would be well served to *aim* for failure. This would, arguably, generate a paradox involving *succeeding* in the attainment of *failure* – or aiming to succeed at an endeavor that *precludes* the possibility of success. If such an effort is not, flat out, incoherent, it at least tends in the general direction of discomfiting cognitive dissonance. Is George Washington less worthy of our respect than is King Leonidas? Both are heroic – but Washington *won*.

Cannot Implies Ought Not

If Immanuel Kant is correct that "ought implies can," then it follows that *cannot* implies *ought* not. This is a fairly straightforward application of *modus tollens* to the sphere of practical reasoning. It is impractical, and arguably incoherent to attempt what cannot be done. That is, one *ought not* attempt the impossible. In any such attempt, the agent wastes time, effort, and resources on a doomed endeavor. Those resources could have, otherwise, been devoted to some project with at least a *hope* of success. How much needless suffering has resulted from failure to desist in hopeless endeavors? Moreover, how much avoidable suffering might have been forestalled by a rational reallocation of the resources wasted in futile pursuits? No exact quantification is possible (any attempt to produce one would be futile), but we may safely conclude that "a lot" would serve as a modest and conservative answer. In *A New Stoicism*, Lawrence Becker articulates the practical and logical problems with futile pursuits:

> The point cannot be more straightforward: We reject the soundness of any normative proposition constructed from an agent's endeavor to do (directly) what she believes to be impossible. We do this because such endeavors are incoherent,

in the sense that their propositional representation always tacitly involves an inconsistent pair of propositions: one about impossibility, to the effect that there are no available means to achieve a given end; the other about a contrary possibility, to the effect that there is a course of conduct that might be a way to achieve the same end... But the system of normative logic constitutes a formal representation of practical reasoning, and practical reasoning aims to resolve such conflict and incoherence. [1998, p. 45]

Practical reasoning cannot countenance the ultimate *impracticality* of applied incoherence. One cannot, as the adage goes, "serve two masters" (one, at least, ought not to attempt to do so), and one certainly cannot abide by inconsistent action-guiding propositions or maxims of conduct. The impossible is, for practical purposes, forbidden to the rational agent.

A Practical Test

The Stoics enjoin us to discontinue any and all concern with, and emotional or psychological attachment to, circumstances or endeavors that are known to be futile, or for which we have reasonably conclusive evidence of futility. This is wise counsel – all too frequently flouted or ignored. Sometimes, there really is no hope. It behooves us to properly identify such cases and respond with rational detachment. What, however, might constitute compelling evidence that any endeavor is, in fact, futile? There are, of course, some fairly obvious cases of physically, nomologically, or logically impossible achievements. These are, however, not *genuine* options of the type William James held up as *live* possibilities. No one sincerely contemplates leaping the Grand Canyon at its widest point, without deploying some form of artificial propulsion. No one thinks, "I will broad jump that distance!" It is clearly impossible for any human to do so. Furthermore, any such attempt, far from being admirable or ennobling, is simply a suicidal exercise in foolishness. This is not an *interesting* case for *practical* counsel. No one needs pronouncements from a Stoic sage to dissuade *obvious* lunacy!

The interesting test case involves the endeavor that is *not* obviously impossible, but that may *appear* to defy reason. What test can distinguish the improbable from the unattainable? How, in actual practice, can one tell the difference? As is often the case with Stoic counsel, the answer is shockingly (and deceptively) simple: Will it to be so. What one's will does not, at the moment in question, produce is, *ipso facto*, beyond the power of one's will – at *that* moment. This may seem a presumptuous determinism and, indeed, it may be. Luckily, practical purposes do not require us to settle recondite metaphysical disputes. Can I control, simply by effort of my will, another person's beliefs, behavior, attitudes, etc.? Those who would answer in the affirmative, thereby, acquire the burden of proof. One may, of course, speak, debate, threaten, and so on. All of these endeavors depend upon the cooperation of one's interlocutor(s). As Epictetus reminds his students, such matters are simply *not* "up to us":

> There are things which are within our power, and there are things which are beyond our power. Within our power are opinion, aim, desire, aversion, and, in one word, whatever affairs are our own. Beyond our power are body, property, reputation, office, and, in one word, whatever are not properly our own affairs. [*Enchiridion*, I]

It is not mere coincidence that Arrian places this *first* on the *Enchiridion*'s list of admonitions to would-be Stoics. This is the *sine qua non* of Epictetan counsel's efficacy. Know what is "yours." Bend *all* of your cognitive efforts on the improvement and perfection of your "internals" (i.e. opinion, aim, desire, aversion, etc.). Know what is *not* yours. Embrace it, accept it, and do not allow yourself to be troubled by anything that is *not* "yours."

Stoic "externals" (i.e. body, property, reputation, office, etc.) are not "up to you," and it is foolish to allow yourself to be concerned about them. Every moment of discontent caused by emotional attachment to the attitudes and behaviors of other persons is a moment that might have been spent improving oneself. We waste our lives insofar as we strive for the unattainable. Life is too short for constructing cloud castles. Our time is too valuable to be frittered away on childish fantasy. Stoicism is largely about embracing the world as it is, and resisting the urge to pine for a world that cannot be.

The Humble Agnostic Shrugs

The robust Muscular Christian haranguing us from the pulpit of my old school chapel admitted a sneaking regard for atheists... What this preacher couldn't stand was agnostics: namby-pamby, mushy pap, weak tea, weedy, pallid fence sitters.
– Richard Dawkins [2006, p. 46]

Agnosticism has fallen again into disfavor in recent days – especially among unbelievers. The thesis is often dismissed as an "easy out" for the wishy-washy, weak-kneed, mush head – or the default position of the merely intellectually slothful sort who simply refuses to think through difficult issues. The agnostic, claim opponents among both believers and their antagonists, simply refuses to embrace the clear implications of the available evidence. It is, they say (or imply), the coward's thesis. It is essentially a mere shrug in the face of controversy. This insistence that we do not (or cannot) know about the existence of God, offered in place of careful critical evaluation, is a sham humility masking unprincipled reticence to truly engage in a contentious and sometimes heated debate. Thus, many in the opposing camps regard agnosticism with contempt, disdain, and derision. Agnostics are, in short, *wimps*.

More Than Not *Knowing*

Stunningly, however, those who so deride agnosticism often, in the very next breath, go on to articulate the agnostic's thesis as an obvious truth. They say (with a hint of disgust), "Of course no one *knows* for certain whether or not there is some kind of god or supernatural phenomenon," as if this somehow undermines agnosticism's credibility as a viable or interesting thesis. In his recent book, *The God Delusion*, Richard Dawkins dismisses agnosticism's foundational claim as a triviality:

That you cannot prove God's non-existence is accepted and trivial, if only in the sense that we can never absolutely prove the non-existence of anything. [2006, p. 54]

How is it, I cannot help but wonder, that a thesis is discredited or deemed trivial simply because it is clearly true? Is the law of non-contradiction similarly trivial and useless? The agnostic, though, has something more to contribute to the debate concerning the existence of the supernatural than merely pointing out that we cannot (or do not) *know with absolute certainty* about the existence of God or gods. This all-too-common mischaracterization of agnosticism is, I shall argue, unfair on several fronts. First, there is nothing inherently counterfeit, intellectually squeamish, or wimpy about the position that we do not know whether some God (or other non-natural entity or force) exists. It is simply an honest recognition of our limitations and/or the intrinsically recondite nature of the subject at hand. Second, the typical agnostic does not merely make a claim about what is or is not *known with certainty*, but argues that we lack sufficient evidence for even embracing belief or disbelief regarding particular propositions. Agnosticism is not wimpy; it is intellectually circumspect and humble – in an arena that calls for a degree of humility. Being only somewhat more intelligent than the other primates, humans ought to embrace the possibility that the foundation of all being could, conceivably, fall beyond our ken. The agnostic simply accepts the possibility that there are some things that we do not know, that we may never know, regarding which we may lack sufficient justification for the formation of any belief at all, and that the nature of ultimately reality could be one such area of inquiry.

Finally, agnosticism is best understood not so much as a thesis one must defend, but rather as a stance issuing a challenge to those brandishing theses regarding the existence or nonexistence of God (or the supernatural). The agnostic does not believe that compelling evidence of (any) God's existence has been offered, and does not believe that compelling evidence has been offered demonstrating that *no* God, creator, designer, or phenomenon transcending the natural realm exists. The agnostic simply sees insufficient justification for adopting a belief in either direction (so to speak), and insists that anyone claiming such justification bears the burden of proof – a burden that has not yet been met to the agnostic's satisfaction. Agnosticism is, I contend, the proper default position regarding God's existence (or the existence of the trans-natural, or non-natural), and judgment about such matters should be withheld unless and until compelling evidence is proffered demonstrating that there either is or is not some type of supernatural phenomenon. It is also worth noting that the locution "some type" is crucial to this dispute. In *The Faith of a Heretic*, Walter Kaufmann notes that:

> The practice of seizing on a label instead of considering a man's ideas is common, if often unconscious. The labels, theist, atheist, and agnostic, provide an especially important example. One supposes that the theist believes God exists, while the atheist denies that God exists, and the agnostic, in the absence of sufficient evidence, suspends judgment. It is further supposed that theists agree about the facts of the matter. One rarely stops to think about what these facts are supposed to be, except, of course, to say that theists think that God exists. But what does this assertion mean? [1961, p. 28]

One must be clear concerning what proposition it is about which one suspends one's judgment. It is important to recognize that there are, and have been, bewilderingly many forms of religious belief. Some of these are undoubtedly worthy of outright rejection and disbelief. Atheism about Thor is, for example, probably quite reasonable. We must, however, be careful about lumping all beliefs concerning the nature of ultimate reality together, and declaring all but the strictly naturalistic equally preposterous. While many conceptions of God or "the divine" may richly deserve the brand of ridicule and disparagement that we find in recent (and admirable) works such as Sam Harris' *The End of Faith*, Christopher Hitchens' *god is not Great*, and Richard Dawkins' *The God Delusion*, it does not follow that every thesis proposing something (or some *non*-thing) other than matter, energy, and natural law ought to be so readily cast aside as the benighted superstition of a pre-scientific age. Though there are a number of theses concerning the nature of God or some transcendence of the natural realm that have not, in my judgment, been demonstrated to be indefensible or absurd, in the interest of parsimony, I will focus on only one hypothesis about which, I shall argue, the proper attitude is the agnostic's suspension of judgment. Let us consider whether there is sufficient evidence for or against *deism*.

Deism: The God Who Does Not Care

The meaning of "deism" that I have in mind here is nicely articulated in Antony Flew's *A Dictionary of Philosophy*. Flew makes the etymological point that the term "deism":

> ... has appeared in various forms in various periods of history, but its best known manifestations are found in the thought of the 18th-century Enlightenment and, especially, of Voltaire. It is usually taken to involve God's leaving the Universe to its own lawful devices, without any particular interventions, once the process of creation had been completed. [1979, p. 87]

It is precisely this non-interventionist aspect of the deistic God (or god – lower case "g") that makes for the difficulty of demonstrating the existence or nonexistence of such a being (or force). Much the same case could be made (though for different reasons) in favor of the agnostic's stance regarding the *Tao* or

Brahman as these are presented within certain Asian wisdom traditions and, perhaps, even some permutations of Stoic conceptions of the all-pervading *Logos*. Let us, however, stick with Voltaire's deism and see if conclusive evidence, or anything like it, can be produced in its favor or against it.

The deist might claim that there is nothing unreasonable about the thesis that God "touched off" the Big Bang ("Let there be light!") and, thereafter, ceased to interact with the universe in any way. Perhaps He, She, or It no longer even notes the passing of events and disinterestedly allows nature to "take its course" whatever that course may be (and whatever consequences might be in store for us). Let us stipulate that no cosmological argument succeeds in proving that such a creator exists (or ever did). Failure to prove the existence of the deistic god does not, however, constitute a proof of that god's *non*existence. It is, as Dawkins suggests, impossible to prove that such a *laissez-faire* god does *not* exist (and never did). This being so, what is the complaint about agnosticism relative to the deistic God? Though questions remain about how such a God (and Its creation) could have come into being, these questions tend to afflict all theories of ultimate origin. Naturalistic accounts of the Big Bang and its causal antecedents also founder (as yet) on the question of cosmological origin.

Generally speaking, the skeptic claims that we do not know a particular proposition or, in many cases, that we are unable even to provide rational justification for any belief regarding the proposition in question. The skeptic's strategy is to demand proof, evidence, argument, or some sort of attempted justification for the interlocutor's hypothesis. The skeptic may then subject the claim in question to rigorous critical evaluation. If the proffered evidence is found wanting, and does not withstand the rigors of skeptical analysis, then the skeptic need not accept the proposition or claim at issue. In such cases, the skeptic simply remains skeptical. To remain skeptical is not necessarily to reject the assertion as false, but simply to insist that it remains unproven (by, at least, the skeptic's lights). The theist, or other believer (there are, after all, non-theistic versions of "the divine" or ultimate reality), must prove that God exists – or *probably* exists. Failing that, it is irresponsible to believe in God. On the other hand, the atheist must demonstrate that we have good reason to believe that *no* God, *no* supernatural or transcendent something-or-other exists – or that it is *probable* that no such thing exists. Failing that, it is irresponsible to embrace atheism.

It is my contention that agnosticism, properly understood, and not atheism, represents the skeptical attitude, and also the most rationally justified position with respect to the question of the existence of God (or gods) as the ultimate creator(s) and/or designer(s) of our universe. Though certain particular conceptions of God may, I think, be safely relegated to the dustbin of religion's often rationally indefensible history, and various particular propositions regarding God's alleged interventions in the (otherwise) natural world (e.g. virgin births, resurrections of the dead, or punitive planetary deluge) may be, indeed *should* be, regarded as almost certainly false (and even embarrassing abjurations of rationality), it does not follow that the possibility of the existence of *any* transcendent grounding of reality has been demonstrated to be irrational.

I do not defend agnosticism regarding anthropomorphisms such as those derived from, for example, a naïve, literalist reading of the Old Testament or the Koran – any more than I would defend agnosticism regarding Thor, Poseidon, Athena, or the Flying Spaghetti Monster. All accounts of such beings are worthy of atheism (i.e. outright rejection) on the grounds that the alleged activities of these beings would constitute contraventions of the established laws of nature. Similarly, any interventionist God (e.g. the type to which one prays) should be regarded as unlikely (to say the least) because the alleged interventions cannot be squared with our most well-confirmed scientific theories. This, however, leaves open the possibility of a non-interventionist or disinterested God (or gods). To put the matter more succinctly, neither the proposition that (some) God exists nor the proposition that no God (of any type) exists have been conclusively established. Shorter still – the deistic god's existence is not obviously more or less probable than that god's nonexistence. If this contention is correct, then the agnostic's "shrug" concerning the matter is the only rationally defensible position. Should one believe that God exists? No. Should one believe that God does not exist? No. What other option is there? One humbly admits that current evidence is insufficient to support either belief – and one leaves it at that.

The Arguments That Need Not Appear Here

Having encountered disturbingly many permutations of cosmological, teleological, and ontological arguments, as well as a dizzying variety of claims to religious or mystical experience (allegedly unexplainable naturalistically) and, having further encountered far more objections to the aforementioned than really ought to have been necessary, it seems to me that the opposition has generally gotten the better of the debate. I will mercifully spare the reader yet another iteration of the interminable explanation of these arguments, objections, replies, counter-replies, etc. Let us assume, for the sake of argument, that all hitherto advanced arguments for God's existence are flawed. Those unwilling to make this assumption, even just for the sake of argument, may find a diminishing marginal utility hereafter. Should I, therefore, adopt the atheist's position and conclude that God does *not* exist? When we add the problem of evil (the scale, scope, intensity, and ubiquity of human suffering) into the mix – another debate into which I will mercifully refrain from wading in this paper – do I not then find that atheistic disbelief remains as the only tenable and, therefore, most rationally justifiable position on the board? Though it may be somewhat unfashionable at the moment to say so, I think not. Merely refuting all available arguments in favor of the existence of a creator and/or designer God(s), and pointing out an apparent problem for one theory of God's nature (namely theism), does not yet amount to a proof of the *nonexistence* (or even the *probable* nonexistence) of a creator and/or designer being (or force, or "transcendent principle," or whatever) underwriting this universe and our presence within it. Unless it can be demonstrated that matter, energy, and the laws of nature are the only plausible antecedents of our presence in this universe, then atheists still, it seems to me, have some work to do.

There are features of the natural world (like the fact that it is here at all, and that it happens to be hospitable to intelligent life), and elements of the human condition that may give (and have given) pause to even cautious, rational observers. Perhaps purely naturalistic explanations of all such phenomena can and ultimately will be given. Perhaps God will prove to be a superfluous posit of a scientifically benighted age. Even so, this would not prove that God (or whatever) does not exist, but would, at most, establish that we, in the words of Pierre Laplace, simply "have no need of that hypothesis." We should not expect this state of affairs to manifest any time soon. The cause (if there was one) of the Big Bang and/or the origin of life might remain forever beyond our reach.

Anticipating Atheist Conniptions

Many atheists will, at this point barely able to contain their derision, impatiently draw analogies to agnosticism about Santa Claus, or about Bertrand Russell's celestial teapot orbiting the sun, unobservable from our vantage point. Such analogies are, however, weak (and, I think, a little disingenuous). Santa and the teapot are much more implausible than the disinterested "first cause" of deism. I am not a scientist, but I am fairly confident that Santa's exploits would constitute violations of a variety of well-established laws of nature. He seems to cover a lot of territory in one night, manages to fit down chimneys that are narrower than himself (not to mention the loot he carries with him), and he is alleged to mush a team of flying reindeer! I will leave it to physicists, engineers, and evolutionary biologists to explain the degree of implausibility inherent in the Santa story. As for Russell's teapot, disbelief is appropriate here as well. There are good reasons to conclude that its occurrence as a natural phenomenon is unlikely in the extreme. There are good reasons to *disbelieve* in both Santa and the teapot. It would be irrational to be "agnostic" about them.

Do we, however, face an analogous proposition in the case of the deistic god? This creator is allegedly responsible for the existence of matter, energy, and the laws of nature that govern them – at least in *this* universe. It would seem, then, that the initial act of creation could not, by the deist's lights, have been subject to, or constrained by, the laws of nature (they weren't "there" yet). Well, it is the laws of nature and the behavior of matter and energy in accordance with those laws that make Santa and Russell's teapot impossible (or, at least, wildly implausible). What then makes it irrational to *refrain from disbelief* in the deistic god? Why is it irrational, when confronted with deism, to simply shrug and admit that it is possible? Why should it be regarded as *obvious* that a purely naturalistic explanation is *more* plausible? An agnostic may legitimately claim to have no justification for embracing the one view as opposed to the other – and may, therefore, refrain from embracing either.

Conclusion

The agnostic demands proof of theses proffered by others brandishing them in the marketplace of ideas. There is a God, you say? Prove it. Provide evidence that your thesis is superior to naturalistic alternatives. There is no God, you say? Prove it. Prove that naturalistic explanations are rationally preferable to all available alternatives. Provide evidence that compels the rational person to disbelieve in all putatively transcendent phenomena. If neither of the competitor theses can meet this challenge (and agnostics are agnostics because neither has met this challenge to their satisfaction), then the only remaining defensible position is a "shrug," and the humble admission that we do not know and, in fact, that we do not even have compelling reason to support either belief or disbelief regarding the competing theses. Sometimes, it must be noted, a shrug really is the best that anyone can do.

Hilbert's Hotel, the Multiverse, and Design

Some physicists solve that problem of the necessity of finely tuned physical constants... by invoking the anthropic principle, saying, well, here we are, we exist, we have to be in the kind of universe capable of giving rise to us. That in itself is, I think, unsatisfying, and as John Lennox rightly says, some physicists solve that by the multiverse idea – the idea that our universe is just one of many universes.
– Richard Dawkins

Our principal result is that the infinite is nowhere to be found in reality. It neither exists in nature nor provides a legitimate basis for rational thought... The role that remains for the infinite to play is solely that of an idea.
– David Hilbert

If Hilbert's Hotel Paradox demonstrates the incoherence of an infinite ensemble of physically instantiated entities, then the "multiverse," postulated as an infinite ensemble of universes, is every bit as incoherent as is Hilbert's Infinite Grand Hotel with its infinite possible guests. Thus, either Hilbert's Hotel Paradox fails to disprove the impossibility of infinite ensembles of physically instantiated entities, or the infinite multiverse cannot exist. If the infinite multiverse does not exist, then the inference to design as the best explanation underpinning our anthropic universe (a universe permitting the development of complex, intelligent beings like ourselves) is significantly strengthened by the elimination of its most compelling competitor thesis. If Hilbert is right our universe is not likely to have arisen from unguided, purely naturalistic causes, laws, constants, or any chance concurrence of spontaneous, unguided conditions.

The Appearance of Fine-Tuning

While the relevant phenomena have been admirably and thoroughly enumerated and explicated elsewhere, it is worth briefly mentioning some of the conditions that appear (at least initially) to be both necessary for the evolution of life, and wildly improbable in the absence of cosmological engineering. Furthermore, the requisite conditions for the evolution of *intelligent*, reasoning creatures such as human beings, *anywhere* in our universe, would appear to be significantly less probable than the conditions required for simpler life forms. Our life-permitting universe and our presence in it as reasoning observers are states of affairs crying out for explanation. William Lane Craig points out some of the phenomena that seem, at first blush, inexplicable without some kind of purposive cosmological engineering:

> The universe appears, in fact, to have been incredibly fine-tuned from the moment of its inception for the production of intelligent life on Earth at this point in cosmic history. In the various fields of physics and astrophysics, classical cosmology, quantum mechanics, and biochemistry, various discoveries have repeatedly disclosed that the existence of intelligent carbon-based life on Earth at this time depends upon a delicate balance of physical and cosmological quantities, such that were any one of these quantities to be slightly altered, the balance would be destroyed and life would not exist. [1990, p. 127]

Much of his subsequent article, "The Teleological Argument and the Anthropic Principle," is devoted to a thorough explication of various features of the cosmos, the biosphere, and human biology that could not plausibly have emerged spontaneously from natural, unguided forces of nature. Furthermore, it is not only theists, such as Craig, who are impressed with the appearance of fine-tuning. Even staunch unbelievers seem generally inclined to admit the initial *appearance* of design, before offering alternative, naturalistic theories to explain *away* the *prima facie* appearances that our universe has been fine-tuned for the evolution of living organisms. Stephen Hawking takes note of some of the appearances in question:

> The remarkable fact is that the values of these numbers [describing fundamental constants, forces, etc.] seem to have been very finely adjusted to make possible the development of life. For example if the electric charge of the electron had been only slightly different, stars either would have been unable to burn hydrogen and helium, or else they would not have exploded. Of course, there might be other forms of intelligent life, not dreamed of even by writers of science fiction, that did not require the light of a star like the sun or the heavier chemical elements that are made in stars and are flung back into space when the stars explode. Nevertheless, it seems clear that there are relatively few ranges of values for the numbers that would allow the development of any form of intelligent life. Most sets of values would give rise to universes that, although they might be very beautiful, would contain no one able to wonder at that beauty. [1988, p. 132]

The cosmological constant, electromagnetic force constant, the strong nuclear force constant, the weak nuclear force constant, and a series of other conditions, must *all* fall within the excruciatingly narrow range in which we find them here in our home universe, if life is to emerge and evolve. Perhaps the most astonishingly improbable of these phenomena is the Penrose number, referring to the initial entropy conditions of the Big Bang. Penrose calculated that the odds against the requisite entropy conditions leading to a life-permitting universe are 10 to the 10^{123}... to one! Paul Davies also describes the strikingly improbable "coincidences" without which there could be no life in our universe. Consider the example of the gravitational constant:

An alteration in, say, the strengths of the gravitational force by a mere one part in 10^{40} would be sufficient to throw out this numerical coincidence. [1983, p. 188]

In each of these cases, and many others that have been noted and explained by experts in the relevant fields [see: Center For Science and Culture, 2015], the requisite conditions for a habitable universe developing without intelligent guidance, or of sufficient orderliness for the evolution of our species, seem to be about as near to impossibility as we can readily imagine. Yet... here we are.

Hilbert's Infinite Hotel

The physical instantiation of an infinite ensemble of entities, as opposed to an infinite ensemble of abstract objects (e.g. numbers), is, according to David Hilbert's oft-cited thought experiment, paradoxical. A fairly standard (and admirably lucid) explication of Hilbert's Hotel Paradox is presented and its implications noted by William Lane Craig:

Let us imagine a hotel with a finite number of rooms. Suppose, furthermore, that *all the rooms are full*. When a new guest arrives asking for a room, the proprietor apologizes, "Sorry, all the rooms are full." But now let us imagine a hotel with an infinite number of rooms and suppose once more that all the rooms are full. There is not a single vacant room throughout the entire infinite hotel. Now suppose a new guest shows up, asking for a room. "But of course!" says the proprietor, and he immediately shifts the person in room #1 into room #2, the person in room #2 into room #3, the person in room #3 into room #4 and so on, out to infinity. As a result of these room changes, room #1 now becomes vacant and the new guest gratefully checks in. But remember, before he arrived, all the rooms were full! Equally curious, according to the mathematicians, *there are now no more persons in the hotel than there were before: the number is just infinite. But how can this be? The proprietor just added the new guest's name to the register and gave him his keys – how can there not be one more person in the hotel than before?*... Can anyone sincerely believe that such a hotel could exist in reality? These sorts of absurdities illustrate the impossibility of the existence of an actually infinite number of things. [1991 – emphasis added]

So, a paradox seems to be generated by the proposition that an infinite ensemble may be physically instantiated. Hilbert's Hotel is only one illustration of a paradox generalizable to any ensemble of an infinite set of physical entities. Note that it is not just the infinite hotel that is logically problematic, but also the infinite number of *persons* inhabiting the hotel. When guests are added, the number of guests does not change – even if the number of new guests is infinite! There is always "room" for an additional infinite set of occupants.

Suppose the "occupants" of the hotel are not persons, but *universes*. There is a universe in each of the infinite rooms. A new universe "shows up." There is *always* more room in the *full* hotel. Does the picture improve if the hotel vanishes? If so, how? The walls, ceilings, and elevators are hardly the problem. It is the infinite ensemble of physically instantiated entities that generates the paradox. It makes no difference whether the putatively infinite set is composed of hotel rooms, persons, or universes. The number of physical entities in any set *must* be finite. Hence, Hilbert's Paradox afflicts the putatively infinite ensemble of universes in the multiverse just as deeply as it afflicts the infinite Grand Hotel and its occupants. If the multiverse is an infinite ensemble of separate spatiotemporal entities, or universes, then the multiverse generates a paradox. This is a more significant problem for multiverse theorists than is the mere absence of positive evidence that the multiverse actually exists – an objection frequently proffered by those antagonistic to the positing of the multiverse as a mechanism for vitiating the apparent improbability of our anthropic universe. Absence of evidence is not, as the old saw goes, evidence of absence. Self-contradictory consequences or inferences are, however, constitutive of a *reductio ad absurdum* against the propositions from which they issue. Not only do we lack evidence that an infinite multiverse does, in fact, exist, we have, if Hilbert's Paradox applies as suggested, an argument that an infinite ensemble of universes *cannot* exist. Of course, the precise nature of the multiverse, as posited and described, will be relevant to any assessment of the argument that Hilbert's Paradox subsumes and precludes the infinite multiverse. So, let us see what the multiverse is supposed to be.

The Infinite Multiverse

The multiverse, as a theoretical posit, takes various forms, but a standard presentation, incorporating its more common features, is offered by Martin Rees in *Before the Beginning: Our Universe and Others*. This universe may be merely an infinitesimal component of an infinite set of disparate universes:

> Our universe may be just one element – one atom, as it were – in an infinite ensemble: a cosmic archipelago. Each universe starts with its own big bang, acquires a distinctive imprint (and its individual physical laws) as it cools, and traces out its own cosmic cycle. The big bang that triggered our entire universe is, in this grander perspective, an infinitesimal part of an elaborate structure that extends far beyond the range of any telescopes. [1998, p. 3]

The infinite variety of universes available within the multiverse renders the existence of a life-permitting, or anthropic, universe far more probable than would the occurrence of our universe as a solitary cosmos. Stephen Hawking explains the relationship between infinite cosmological possibilities, and the apparent improbability of an anthropic universe:

> If the universe is indeed spatially infinite, or if there are infinitely many universes, there would probably be some large regions somewhere that started out in a smooth and uniform manner... At first sight this might seem very improbable, because such smooth regions would be heavily outnumbered by chaotic and irregular regions. However, suppose that only in the smooth regions were galaxies and stars formed and were conditions right for the development of complicated self-replicating organisms like ourselves who were capable of asking the question: Why is the universe so smooth? This is an example of the application of what is known as the anthropic principle, which can be paraphrased as "We see the universe the way it is because we exist." [1988, p. 130]

The apparent fine-tuning of our universe for life is explained *away* as an artifact of infinite "trial" universes (or regions of one infinite universe). No matter what the apparent improbability of the conditions for life, it is, nonetheless, bound to emerge in at least one of an infinite set of cosmological possibilities with infinitely many differing initial conditions. As we have seen, however, an *infinite* ensemble of universes is subject to Hilbert's Paradox (as is an infinite set of regions *within* one universe). An *infinite* multiverse is logically problematic. Indeed, an infinite set of physically instantiated entities of any kind, in any bounded or unbounded region, may constitute a logical absurdity akin to a square circle, or a set containing all sets that are not members of themselves. Improbabilities weighed against infinite possibilities might become more plausible (though not at all *entailed* – as there could be *any* number of non-anthropic universes), but if infinite ensembles of universes are not realizable in physical reality, naturalism loses its most potent alternative to the design hypothesis. Other possibilities remain, of course. Our anthropic universe *could* be astronomically improbable *and* a manifestation of pure, unguided chance. That is *conceivable*. It is also possible that there is some purely naturalistic principle of spontaneous order remaining as yet undiscovered by our most advanced sciences, instrumentation, etc. Perhaps any physically instantiated universe is bound to be life-permitting due to some natural cosmological phenomenon that is, by its very nature (or by the very nature of any potential observers), inherently undetectable. Other possibilities can also be conjured with a bit of ingenuity. Are any of these possibilities, given our current understanding, *obviously* more plausible than the hypothesis that our universe *appears* to be fine-tuned for life because it, in fact, *is* fine-tuned for life? The burden of proof in these matters is, at the very least, disputable.

The Finite Multiverse

If Hilbert's thought experiment precludes the possibility of an infinite ensemble of physical entities, then the number of universes must be finite. Perhaps our universe is the only one that exists. In that case, the appearance of design is difficult, if not impossible to dispel. If, however, the number of universes in the multiverse is finite, but sufficiently large (let us use the term "very large" to designate a sufficiently numerous set of universes), then naturalistic explanation for our anthropic universe may still be viable – provided that the total number of universes is sufficiently large to counterbalance the aforementioned improbabilities that appear to be requisite for the evolution of intelligent life. Apart from an *ad hoc* effort to undercut the inference to design, what positive reason can be offered for supposing the finite number of universes to be sufficiently large for a plausible naturalistic explanation for our anthropic universe as (at least) one member of the ensemble? William Lane Craig argues that we are faced with a basic dichotomy regarding plausible explanations:

> But why should we think that the number of universes is actually infinite? This is by no means inevitable, not to mention the paradoxical nature of the existence of an actually infinite number of things. And why should we think that the multiple universes are exhaustively random? Again, this is not a necessary condition of many-worlds hypotheses. In order to elude the teleological argument, we are being asked to assume much more than the mere existence of multiple universes...
>
> We appear then to be confronted with two alternatives: posit either a cosmic Designer or an exhaustively random, infinite number of other worlds. Faced with these options, is not theism just as rational a choice as multiple worlds? [1988, p. 395]

It is, of course, *conceivable* that the multiverse includes a finite, but sufficiently "very large," set of universes for at least one anthropic universe to develop without any intelligent design underpinning its presence within the ensemble of other universes. Keep in mind, however, that the Penrose number, alone, requires the multiverse to contain at least 10 to the 10^{123} universes just to offset the improbability of our universe's initial entropy conditions. The insistence that the multiverse *must* be so or, indeed, that it is *probably* so appears without further argument to be nothing more than an *ad hoc* bit of desperation intended to forestall an inference to design. The multiverse is finite but *surely* it is "large enough" to warrant naturalistic explanations for our anthropic universe. Why should we believe this to be "surely" so? Is it because spontaneous, unguided order of this magnitude is, otherwise, implausible? Perhaps. That hardly justifies the presumption of a sufficiently "very large" multiverse. Furthermore, we are still left with unanswered questions about why the "very large" ensemble of universes should not all be identical, or similar to one another insofar as being devoid of organic structures is concerned. There is nothing incoherent about innumerably many universes containing nothing but inorganic matter, governed by natural laws that are never conducive to the evolution of even the simplest forms of life. Why is a "very large" multiverse containing at least one anthropic universe more probable than a "very large" multiverse containing no such universe, and no observers or minds capable of wondering how they got there? A grand ensemble of universes without anyone to wonder about any of it is no less a possibility, and no less *obviously* probable, than is the alternative with which we seem to be presented in our actual world. So…why *are* we here? Is our world produced by a "very large," unguided multiverse, one or more designers, or some as-yet-unspecified (but plausible) alternative? I confess ignorance as to what exactly recommends the first of those alternatives as more plausible than the second.

Conclusion

The multiverse cannot consist of an *infinite* ensemble of universes, any more than Hilbert's Hotel can coherently house an infinite contingent of guests. Thus, the multiverse can only provide a plausible explanation for our anthropic universe occurring spontaneously, or without intelligent design, if it is sufficiently "very large" to offset the naturalistic improbabilities apparent in the agonizingly narrow ranges in which our universe's fundamental constants, forces, and initial conditions *must* be found. There is no obvious justification for supposing the set of universes composing the multiverse to be sufficiently large to warrant the inference that our anthropic universe arose spontaneously – unless we insist that it *must* be so, in order to avoid an inference to intelligent design. Clearly, this is simply an *ad hoc*, question-begging maneuver on the part of those who regard intelligent design as anathema. It is one thing to despise the idea of intelligent design. It is something else entirely to offer a viable theoretical alternative. Until a viable, purely naturalistic alternative is proffered, the intelligent design theorist is not required, by any rational principle, to abandon the inference that the *appearance* of design results, quite probably, from intelligent, purposive fine-tuning of our universe. A designer is, at present, at least as reasonable an explanation for our universe as is any version of the multiverse yet conceived by our best cosmologists. Design is *not* incompatible with our best science.

Divine Fiat and Blind Obedience

But who are you, a human being, to talk back to God? Shall what
is formed say to the one who formed it, "Why did you make me like
this?"
– Romans 9:17–20

Why do you call me, "Lord, Lord," and do not do what I say?
– Luke 6:46

If there is a God, a Creator or Designer of the universe, and of
all conditions that allow for intelligent life, then God, I shall
argue, can impose *any* moral laws at all within His creation.
This is, at first glance, an odd undertaking for someone, such
as myself, who lacks belief in both God and moral facts. I am
not convinced that we can make sense of moral facts, and I am
not convinced that there is an intelligent Creator or Designer of
the universe. The absence of commitment to moral or religious
dogma may serve to forestall suspicions of naked partisanship
or theological intransigence underlying the project of defending
Divine Command Theory (or so one may, at least, hope). In any
event, I will make the case that the unalloyed "bullet biting"
response, offered by William of Ockham and others, to standard
objections against Divine Command Theory is not, inherently,
any more problematic than similar defenses of Kantian
deontology, utilitarianism, or other mainstream moral theories.
Divine Command Theory may well be entirely wrong, either for
lack of a Divine Commander, or for other reasons entirely, but it
is no more *obviously* wrong, or inherently untenable than are any
of its competitor theories. Contrary to the popular contention
that the Socratic confutation of Divine Command Theory in the
Euthyphro put to rest any serious or worthwhile debate about
its viability, the Divine Command Theorist can, without shame

or dissimulation, cleave to the doctrine that moral goodness is, fundamentally, a matter of naked obedience to divine authority. If God made *everything*, and if there are moral laws, then God made *them* as well. Divine fiat is *no less* defensible a foundation for morality than is the categorical imperative or the principle of utility. For moral skeptics (such as myself), the previous sentence constitutes something less than a ringing endorsement of Divine Command Theory, and something more than vague skepticism regarding alternatives.

The *Euthyphro* Dilemma

Divine Command Theory is, at root, the contention that God commands morally good actions and attitudes, whereas God forbids morally evil actions and attitudes. That, alone, is only the assertion of a *correlation* between moral facts and God's commands. There are, at least, two possible explanations for this correlation. Perhaps God infallibly commands behaviors that are good *independently* of God's will and infallibly forbids behaviors that are independently evil. Let us refer to this version of Divine Command Theory as *Divine Infallibility Theory*. If this is the relationship between God's commands and morality, the Divine Command Theorist owes an account of the non-divine source of moral facts, and an explanation of what it is, if it is *not* God's will, that makes the morally good actions good, and the morally evil actions evil. If God commands, for example, honoring one's mother and father, and if God forbids, for example, murder, because they are, respectively, morally good, and morally evil, *independently* of His will, then we have an explanation for *why* God *commands* the former and *forbids* the latter, but we have been given no explanation of *why* the former *is* morally good, or *why* the latter *is* morally evil. Thus, Divine Command Theorists are generally disinclined to defend the Divine Infallibility version of Divine Command Theory.

If, on the other hand, God's will, simply *by virtue* of the fact that it is *God's* will, *makes* certain behaviors morally good, and other behaviors morally evil, then we have our explanation for the *origin* or *foundation* of moral facts. In *Super 4 Libros Sententiarum*, William of Ockham argues that God's commands are morally self-justifying. God commands, and we are, thereby, morally obligated to obey. Moral facts "spring into existence," as did the rest of God's creation, by divine *fiat*. Let us refer to *this* account of the relationship between God's commands and moral facts as *Divine Fiat Theory* (hereafter, DFT). Thus, according to DFT, God simply *made* the act and attitude of honoring one's mother and father morally good *by virtue of issuing the command* to honor one's parents, whereas God simply *made* murder morally evil *by virtue of issuing the injunction against* committing murder. In this case, we have an explanation for the existence of moral facts, but we are left with no explanation of, or independent justification for, God's *issuing* of commands at all, and no explanation for His issuing of the *specific* commands that we find "on the books" (or, perhaps, in *The* Book). In other words, we are given no reason *why* God forbids, for example, murder. It is *not* because murder was, or is, evil independently of God's will, and was thus forbidden by the infallible issuer of moral commands. That would be the explanation proffered by those who embrace Divine Infallibility Theory. Why, however, should He who created *everything* need an "independent" justification for anything? Indeed, is the concept of an *independent* justification even coherent in this case?

According to DFT, there can be no appeal to moral good or evil obtaining independently of God's will. Does this render morality arbitrary? Suppose that, contrary to *forbidding* murder, God had commanded us *to commit* murder (or rape, or torture, etc.). DFT seems to entail that murder, as well as any other horrifyingly cruel behavior at all, would have been *morally good*, had God commanded us to *commit* murder (or rape, etc.). Those who, for this reason, reject (indeed, *dismiss*) DFT typically argue that murder, rape, torture, genocide, and the rest, *cannot* be morally good, cannot *have been* morally good, under *any* circumstances, and thus moral facts *cannot* be determined solely by divine fiat or God's commands. Michael W. Austin's entry in the *Internet Encyclopedia of Philosophy* is about as good a summary as any for an accessible synopsis of this "second horn" of the *Euthyphro* dilemma:

> The dialogue between Socrates and Euthyphro is nearly omnipresent in philosophical discussions of the relationship between God and ethics... For our purposes, it will be useful to rephrase Socrates' question. Socrates can be understood as asking "Does God command this particular action because it is morally right, or is it morally right because God commands it?" It is in answering this question that the divine command theorist encounters a difficulty. A defender of Divine Command Theory might respond that an action is morally right because God commands it. However, the implication of this response is that if God commanded that we inflict suffering on others for fun, then doing so would be morally right. We would be obligated to do so, because God commanded it. This is because, on Divine Command Theory, the reason that inflicting such suffering is wrong is that God commands us not to do it. However, if God commanded us to inflict such suffering, doing so would become the morally right thing to do. The problem for this response to Socrates' question, then, is that God's commands and therefore the foundations of morality become arbitrary, which then allows for morally reprehensible actions to become morally obligatory. [August 21, 2006]

According to objections against DFT, God's commands are *arbitrary*, and morality would be grounded in nothing more than the divine *whim*. God could, in principle, have commanded *anything*, and could have forbidden *anything* (e.g. kindness, compassion, generosity, etc.). Detractors insist that being virtuous, behaving in morally appropriate fashion, simply *cannot* be a matter of bare, blind obedience to authority, irrespective of the nature of the prescriptions and proscriptions issued by that authority. Virtue *cannot* be simply a matter of doing what one is commanded to do – no matter *who* issues the commands. Our intuitions cannot be reconciled with morality as blind obedience. One must have some independent moral justification for obeying orders. Absent such a moral justification, there is nothing virtuous or admirable about mere obedience to authority.

There may well be ample *prudential* justification for obedience to a God who has the power to impose the most horrific tortures imaginable (and perhaps some that transcend our limited human imagination) upon the disobedient, but obedience motivated by self-interest, by the desire to avoid punishment and, perhaps, obtain reward, is not morally good or virtuous obedience. Such obedience is servile, unreflective, and cowardly. We have no justification for *admiring* the servile, thoughtless coward – even if we understand and forgive cowardice in the face of the ultimate threat to life, limb, soul, loved ones, and everything that one could ever value. Blind obedience is no virtue, and fiat, even *ultimate* fiat, is no foundation for moral decency. Divine Command Theory, therefore, founders on either horn of the *Euthyphro* dilemma and, thus, fails. I contend, however, that DFT has been dismissed with undue, anthropocentric haste. Let us assume that God's commands are, in fact, "arbitrary" (insofar as they are not dependent upon any objective state of affairs other than God's will), and that morality is, therefore, grounded in nothing more than servility before divine whim. It is not at all obvious that obedience to the *ultimate* authority is a uniquely indefensible foundation for a moral theory. Moral facts, *if* they exist (or obtain), must be grounded in *something* and, if God created *everything* (apart from *Himself*), then the ultimate moral "wellspring" may as well be God as any other source. Indeed, a creator God would, arguably, *have* to serve the role of moral foundation.

Where Were *You*?

The eponymous Job, of the *Torah*, believed that his suffering was not justified or, at the very least, that the justification for his suffering had not been satisfactorily explained. He demanded that God defend Himself. Not surprisingly, given much of what we are told about His previous Biblical exploits, God is not inclined gracefully to suffer demands from His children. By what ungrateful temerity, God wonders aloud (we imagine *thunderously* so), does this mere *man*, this creature of His making, inhabiting a world of His making, dare to demand *anything* from his Creator? Job's life is thus, because God has *made* it thus (or *allowed* it to *become* thus). The creature complains of his suffering? God's creation is, literally, *not good enough* for Job? The world is not (currently) to Job's liking – though, it may be noted, Job had not complained of his previous state of health, wealth, and happiness. God is not amused by Job's audacity:

> Then the Lord spoke to Job out of the storm. He said: "Who is this that obscures my plans with words without knowledge? Brace yourself like a man; I will question you, and you shall answer me. Where were you when I laid the earth's foundation? Tell me, if you understand." [Job 38:1–4]

God makes a point of stressing the hierarchical nature of the relationship between Job and Himself. God says, "*I* will question *you*, and you shall answer *me*." In other words, do *not* presume to make demands of *me*, your Creator. I will make demands of *you* – and you will have no say in the matter. Your place, Job, is to endure, *obey*, and be *grateful* in your *servility*. Job, it seems, gets the message:

Then Job replied to the Lord: "I know that you can do all things; no purpose of yours can be thwarted. You asked, 'Who is this that obscures my plans without knowledge?' Surely I spoke of things I did not understand, things too wonderful for me to know. You said, 'Listen now, and I will speak; I will question you, and you shall answer me.' My ears had heard of you but now my eyes have seen you. Therefore I despise myself and repent in dust and ashes." [Job 46:1–6]

Job repents of his arrogance and ingratitude – in dust (whence God *made* man) and ashes. Who, after all, does Job think he is? Parents have, for ages, responded similarly to griping, ungrateful children – and God's authority over humankind far outstrips the human parent's authority over any (mere) biological offspring. Where, indeed, were "we" when God laid *all* foundations? If the moral law does not "sit well" with "us," an omniscient being cannot be expected, therefore, to question or modify His judgment. Indeed, it may not be *coherent* for an omniscient being to do so.

Divine Fiat and Moral Intuition

The specific judgments entailed by the commands of a seemingly perverse, malevolent, or inscrutable God (e.g. commit genocide, take slaves, refrain from compassion, etc.) may be radically counterintuitive. This problem is not, however, unique to DFT. Kantian deontologists struggle to explain radically counterintuitive applications of the categorical imperative (e.g. the obligation to tell the truth to an assassin at the door), and utilitarian theorists have not fared much better with objectionable applications of the principle of utility (e.g. the obligation to kill one's own child so as to save five complete strangers). There is, of course, *no* moral theory against which seemingly insoluble objections have not been raised. This is just one reason that moral skepticism persistently nags at the periphery of nearly all debates concerning good and evil.

Some will argue that DFT suffers from a "deeper" or more foundational flaw than its competitors. Irrespective of *specific* unpalatable commands, the very *concept* of bare fiat as the grounding of moral fact strikes some as a nonstarter. Whatever it is that distinguishes the morally good from the morally evil, it simply *cannot* be the mere fact that someone, *anyone*, just *says so*. DFT is especially problematic if God is not, Himself, virtuous on grounds independent of His own will. Surely, this has something to do with Robert Adams' attempt to modify Divine Command Theory *given* the presumption of a *loving* God, who commands only that which is *good for* his beloved children, and forbids only that which is detrimental to them (*all* things considered – from an *omniscient* perspective). Adams' modification is interesting, and I offer no critique of it here, apart from suggesting that God's benevolence or love for human beings is not *necessary* for an internally consistent theory of morality by Divine Fiat. There is nothing incoherent or indefensible about the contention that moral facts are *whatever* God *damn well* says they are. Suppose God had commanded genocide (and see Deuteronomy 7:1–2 and 20:16–18 for the suggestion that He *did*). According to DFT, any genocide God commands *is* morally good precisely *because* God ordered "his people" to commit it. What God commands is *ipso facto* morally obligatory. If we all owe God our lives, our very existence in a universe of His creation, why would He not have the moral authority to deal with us in whatever manner He pleases?

That suggestion may be shockingly counterintuitive. Whether it is a more difficult pill to swallow than many judgments into which we are driven by Aristotelian, Kantian, or utilitarian reasoning is, to say the least, disputable. If, however, God *literally* created the perpetrators, the victims, and the entire world in which the genocide is prescribed, it is less than obvious that our (mere) human intuitions should trump God's commands. Job's

God is not impressed with human intuition. His purposes are, after all, "too wonderful" for Job (or any of us) to know.

Blind Obedience and Pit Bulls

Some pit bulls are trained to attack *on command*. A well-trained attack dog (a *good* one) unhesitatingly obeys its master's command to attack. That command justifies the attack within the context of this relationship, and the pit bull is in no position to evaluate the legitimacy of any particular attack command. This, at least, is the assessment of the *master fiat theory* of pit bull propriety. The master *owns* the dog, feeds the dog, may have bred the dog, and generally sustains the animal in every significant respect. In return, the master expects blind obedience. Might the master order the pit bull to attack an innocent person, or order it to fight another pit bull for the master's entertainment? The master might – and what of it? The rest of us may pass judgment against the cruel or sadistic dog owner. We, after all, are capable of the sort of reasoning requisite for such evaluations (or, at least, we tend to *believe* that we are), whereas the dog is clearly not. Does it follow that persons are equipped to assess God's commands in the same way that we might assess the sadism or cruelty of the malevolent pit bull owner? God's superiority to humankind (with respect to any relevant properties one might choose), presumably, exceeds our superiority to our canine companions.

Conclusion

The assertion that persons *are*, in fact, equipped to pass moral judgment on, or against, God's commands simply begs the question against DFT. Reason must appeal to some standard *other than* God's fiat for a morally or rationally justifiable rejection of God's commands. Clearly, any such appeal *presumes* that which an objection against DFT is obligated to *prove* – specifically, the existence of an objective moral standard, independent of God's will. DFT's opponents must demonstrate that there *must be*, or at least that there *is*, a moral standard independent of God's commands, and that human reason or intuition can, in principle, access that independent standard. God's commands may be cruel, sadistic, genocidal, etc., but they cannot fail to determine moral facts if, as DFT contends, God's injunctions *make* that which is commanded morally good, and that which is forbidden morally evil. How could God be subject to a "higher standard" of morality? If there is a God, then the moral facts are whatever God damn well says they are. This may excite a bit of skepticism regarding *both* God *and* moral facts, but the Divine Command Theorist need not retreat from DFT as a viable response to the *Euthyphro* dilemma, or complaints of an "arbitrary" moral foundation. Who, after all, are *you*... to "talk back" to God?

Stoic Suicide: Death Before Dishonor

There is but one truly serious philosophical problem, and that is suicide. Judging whether life is or is not worth living amounts to answering the fundamental question of philosophy.
– Albert Camus [1955, p. 3]

Above all, remember that the door stands open. Be not more fearful than children; but as they, when they weary of the game, cry, "I will play no more," even so, when thou art in the like case, cry, "I will play no more" and depart. But if thou stayest, make no lamentation.
– Epictetus, *The Golden Sayings of Epictetus*

I suppose that ye also have decided to detain in life by force a man as old as I am, and to sit by him in silence and keep watch of him: or are ye come with the plea that it is neither shameful nor dreadful for Cato, when he has no other way of salvation, to await salvation at the hands of his enemy?
– Cato the Younger

Suicide is regarded, generally, as tragic – perhaps understandable in some circumstances, perhaps defensible on the odd occasion, and perhaps even morally justifiable on the rare occasion. Faced with conditions *in extremis*, the standard presumptions may not apply, and intentionally taking one's own life may be the lesser of the available evils. The presumption, however, remains that suicide is *prima facie* impermissible, and is, at best, a tragedy. In this paper, I hope to challenge that presumption, and explain the Roman Stoic criteria for a defensible, perhaps even noble, suicide. I shall argue that suicide is, given the correct circumstances, not merely permissible, but that it is morally preferable, on multiple fronts, to the available alternatives, including survival until natural death or some involuntary end to the rational agent's life. Indeed, the expression "natural" death may serve to prejudice moral evaluations of alternatives such as suicide, as they are likely to be deemed *unnatural* by comparison, and "unnatural" carries connotations of perversity or impropriety (as in "unnatural" sexual acts). Perhaps natural death, or continued life until involuntary death, may reasonably be regarded as unpalatable, if continued existence is ignominious, continuous dissolution, or if it necessitates degradation by one's own lights. Might it not be true that maintaining one's decency could literally require "death before dishonor," as the ancient Roman slogan, and contemporary US Marine motto, suggests? Suicide, the voluntary determination of (ideally) the time, place, and manner of one's death, has had its name dragged through the rhetorical mud for too long and with insufficient dispassionate reflection. So, I hereby rise in defense of the supposed anathema of suicide, and I hope to contribute somewhat to the rehabilitation of "death before dishonor" as a noble Stoic injunction. A pointless persistence unto decrepitude may well constitute the type of dishonor that is unpalatable to Stoic sensibilities.

Stoicism and Justifiable Suicide

The Roman Stoics seem to have agreed that there are many fates worse than death and, more to our current point, a number of fates that warrant suicide in lieu of continued existence in a condition of degeneracy or dishonor (though there appears to have been some disagreement concerning the necessary and sufficient conditions for legitimately taking one's own life). If a virtuous life in accordance with reason and decency is no longer possible, or if continued survival necessitates disgrace, or obeisance to indefensible persons or values, then most of the Stoics seem to have agreed that death is, in such instances, a lesser evil than an unproductive or otherwise shameful life. Epictetus tells us that:

> Men are disturbed, not by things, but by the principles and notions which they form concerning things. *Death*, for instance, is *not* terrible, else it would have appeared so to Socrates. But the terror consists in our notion of death that it is terrible. [*Enchiridion*, 5 – emphasis added]

Socrates, a hero and moral exemplar for Epictetus and the other Stoics (not to mention devotees of other Hellenistic schools), regarded death as a lesser evil than cowardice, criminality, impiety, or other forms of vice and degradation. It is crucial to note that Socrates chose death even though the option of survival in exile was, by all accounts, available to him. Life as a cowardly, impious criminal "on the run" was, in Socrates' estimation, a life not worth living, and a greater evil than death by drinking hemlock – as Socrates explained during his trial [*Apology*, 29–30]. Although Socrates' death is correctly described as an execution, rather than a suicide, that distinction is not crucial to the question of whether persisting in degradation is sufficient cause to choose death (by execution, suicide, or some other means) rather than a life continued at the expense of one's dignity, or at the cost of abandoning one's moral rectitude. If the price of continued life is ignominy, vice, or moral lassitude, the price is too high, and it is time to take to Epictetus' "open door" without complaint or regret. We must take full responsibility for our choice to "leave or remain," and embrace the conditions attendant upon that choice. If the option is death or dishonor, death or degradation, death or self-abasement, then the Stoic and Socratic advice is to choose death with a clear conscience.

What, however, if the option is death or disrepair, death or debilitation, death or decrepitude – a literal "sickness unto death" with no viable hope of recovery or improvement? Illness or injury *can* impose constraints upon agency, and diminished capacities, that are incompatible with a life of reason and virtue. Is there a rational justification for persisting in a life of decay and decline, or a life that is devoid of any plausible purpose or goal beyond *persistence itself*? The Stoic lives for the pursuit of wisdom and virtue. Once these pursuits become impossible, life's purpose is lost. Life without the capacity for active reasoning and striving toward self-improvement may be fit for dogs or pigs, but a Stoic should have none of it. When reason fails irrecoverably, or the body becomes permanently incapable of translating reason into action, "opting out" need not be regarded as tragic or cowardly. Indeed, it may be the only dignified act left to a reasoning, virtuous agent.

Non-Injurious Death: Lives Not Worth Living

Anyone unwilling to contemplate the possibility that a human life might cease to be worth living, irrespective of surrounding circumstances, will be inclined to dismiss my thesis as intuitively implausible, and will likely find my arguments less than compelling. The inalienable and/or incorrigible value of all human life irrespective of circumstance is, however, a fairly difficult position, upon analysis, to defend. Some lives are so filled with persistent suffering, or so devoid of purpose, significance, or hope, that any attempt to insist that persons are obligated to persist in their irremediably unenviable condition seems inhumane to the point of cruelty. For some, the condition of persistent purposelessness, real or perceived, constitutes an emotional, spiritual, or moral condition rendering life devoid of meaning or value. Such a life may be regarded as degrading, unworthy of living, and even inherently dishonorable. Declining to indulge in dishonor is no vice. In the context of discussing the morality of euthanasia, Richard Brandt offers the following scenario as an example of *non-injurious* killing:

> What might be a noninjurious killing? If I come upon a cat that has been mangled but not quite killed by several dogs and is writhing in pain, and if I pull myself together and

put it out of its misery, I have killed the cat but surely not *injured* it. I do not injure something by relieving its pain. If someone is being tortured and roasted to death and I know he wishes nothing more than a merciful termination of life, I have not injured him if I shoot him; I have done him a favor. In general, it seems I have not injured a person if I treat him in a way in which he would want me to treat him if he were fully rational, or in a way to which he would be indifferent if he were fully rational. [1975, p. 153]

Much as one does the mangled cat no injury by euthanizing it quickly and (relatively) painlessly, one does oneself no injury by departing a situation in which noble, decent conduct is no longer a viable option. Thus, the non-injurious suicide is conceivable. The Stoic disdains stagnation and decline. One section of Epictetus' *Discourses*, entitled, "How One May Be True To One's Character In Everything," begins with an exhortation to consider suicide when "it is rational," and death has become more "attractive" than continued life in unacceptable circumstances:

To the rational creature that which is against reason is alone past bearing; the rational he can always bear. Blows are not by nature intolerable.

"What do you mean?"

Let me explain; the Lacedaemonians bear flogging, because they have learnt that it is in accord with reason.

"But is it not intolerable to hang oneself?"

At any rate, when a man comes to feel that it is *rational*, he goes and hangs himself at once. [Chapter II – emphasis added]

If the concept of a life not worth living, or well worth *ending*, is coherent, then the option of suicide is, at the very least, a potentially defensible proposition. Even opponents of euthanasia will admit that some lives can become a disvalue to those living them. Such lives may be regarded as exceptional cases upon which it is ill advised to construct general maxims about the value of life. Those lives are, nonetheless, difficult to regard as chimerical or fictitious. Indeed, they may not be so rare as some assume.

Suppose that an individual deems his probable future experiences to be, on the whole, not worth living. If there is compelling evidence that one's life is entirely (if the euphemism may be forgiven) "downhill from here," then there is a *prima facie* case for evading one's painful, humiliating, or otherwise unenviable future via the most expedient available course of action. In short, if one's future is not worth having, then it may be entirely rational to choose not to experience it. We may, at least, insist that the burden of proof is to be borne by those who would argue that one bears an obligation to persist in living a life for which all available evidence indicates a sustained downward hedonic gradient, and a declining utility in all other respects with which one might plausibly be concerned (e.g. intellectual dissolution, diminishing utility to one's family, society, etc.). Why should we continue to anathematize a rational choice to desist in a life that is, on the whole, burdensome to all concerned (or, at least, to all those with whom one is most intimately and centrally concerned)? Perhaps there is such a thing as a noble and non-injurious exit from a life that is no longer worth living. Perhaps a case can be made that one dishonors oneself by persisting as a decrepit burden or a malignancy with which others must contend.

Cato's Suicide
NS Gill begins "The Suicide of Cato the Younger" with this

description of Cato's character and his death:

> A defender of the Roman Republic, he forcefully opposed Julius Caesar and was known as the highly moral, incorruptible, inflexible supporter of the Optimates. When it became clear at the Battle of Thapsus... that Julius Caesar would be the political leader of Rome, Cato chose the philosophically accepted way out, suicide. [2017]

If Cato was, in fact, "highly moral" and "incorruptible," does his suicide make him any less so? He chose not to accede to Caesar's alleged authority to issue him a pardon, and, thereby, avoid acquiescence to tyranny. Cato chose death before dishonor. Should we regard Cato's final act as an ignominious departure from a life of moral rectitude? A good case can be made that we should not. Life as a submissive vassal prostrating himself before the power of Julius Caesar, a life entailing cowardice, treason, and an irreversible abdication of his role as defender of the Roman Republic, did not satisfy Cato. A morally dissolute persistence in a condition of servility was not a life worthy of the great man's continued participation. Indeed, such a life would have been antithetical to his most central and most prized values. To exist as a useless adjunct to an empire ruled by a tyrant, and to do so in an attitude of malignancy and disgust, would have been treasonous, intolerable, and contemptible in Cato's estimation. A vile existence, a life that turns the stomach of the agent living it, is not worthy of that agent's continued participation. The only noble, admirable choice remaining is departure. The departure cannot be only geographical or merely a matter of retreat into hermitage. Voluntarily leaving the empire would not have assuaged Cato's experience of his own failure, his own acquiescence to tyranny and abandonment of the remaining Roman citizens, or his own assessment that it would be treasonous and cowardly to remain alive while Rome falls under the thumb of a despot. When life itself is the problem, when continuing in an intolerable and irredeemable existence *is* the dishonor one is morally compelled to avoid, then death is the only available cure for this malady of the conscience. When the cure is readily available, it is irrational and ignoble to persist in a life to which one's conscience cannot be reconciled. One need not be a Cato standing athwart a Julius Caesar's tyrannical plans in order that one's persistence in a life not worth living might constitute sufficient cause to *end* it. One may face a future of physical decline, intellectual deterioration, burdensomeness, and moral malignancy in one's own estimation. If those to whom one owes one's greatest fealty are precisely those for whom one's persistence will be the most onerous, then a case can be made for choosing death as the only remaining salvation.

Dissolution and Dishonor

Most of us believe that we do our pets no injury by having them humanely "put to sleep" (a euphemism for *put to death*) when they have incontrovertibly crossed a certain threshold relative to future enjoyments (or the lack thereof), and face hedonic, physical, and other forms of decline until a natural death will finally end their valueless, persistent suffering. We bring our pets to the veterinarian for euthanasia because we love them and hope to spare them a slow, lingering death following an extended and painful disintegration. What reason, then, can be proffered for refusing to provide our human loved ones the same option of escape from a hideous and degrading future? Without a moral, or otherwise compelling obligation to persist in an undesirable existence to the "bitter end" (a telling expression), we are owed an argument for abridging or anathematizing the exercise of individual and bodily autonomy expressed through the act of suicide. A rational agent who finds neither purpose nor value in living any longer does not perpetrate any obvious evil by voluntarily ceasing to do so. We do not (generally) accept any moral obligation to marry, procreate, accept religious dogma, or undertake any other activity to which one does not consent. Why should we hold a different attitude toward the various activities that constitute the enterprise of living a life from which one has withdrawn consent? Much as each of us remains morally free to withdraw from marriage, citizenship, membership in a religious community or political party, and even to renounce parental rights (given proper justification), each of us, similarly, retains the right to withdraw from existence in this "vale of tears" (another interesting euphemism). If Cato's preference for suicide, rather than subservience to a tyrant, is defensible, or plausibly regarded as an admirable final act of autonomy and rebellion against authoritarianism, then a case can be made for opting out of the "tyranny" of disease, dissolution, and irreversible decline. Might any of us not ask, as did Cato:

> When and where, without my knowledge, have I been adjudged a madman... but I am prevented from using my own judgement... that Caesar may find me unable to defend myself when he comes? [Gill, 2017]

If it is not Caesar, but rather dissolution or decrepitude that "comes for me," should I not "use my own judgement" in facing my adversary?

If reason and experience inform me that I am "better off dead," then a compelling argument (and not mere presumption or dogmatic insistence) is needed to demonstrate the falsity of that proposition (i.e. that I am *not*, in fact, better off dead), or that I am obligated to continue living even though I *am*, in fact, better off dead. Demonstrating either proposition is, at least in many instances, bound to be a fairly tall order. Assuming that I am "in my right mind," who is in a better position than myself to render judgment as to the probable overall value of my continued existence? Assuming that I bear no overriding special duty to persist for the sake of particular others (e.g. my underage children), why, and to whom, would I owe an obligation to keep living, even if the cessation of my existence is preferable by my own lights? If I retain the autonomy to do what I want with my body and my life, provided that my actions do not impinge upon the rights or liberties of others, then it is very difficult to justify the claim that the act of suicide should fall outside the scope of that autonomy. My death is, in the first instance, *my* business and, in many cases, my final opportunity to make a crucial decision about what to do with my life – which includes the decision to *end* it. A life that can no longer conform to my values and my conception of a worthy endeavor is a life unworthy of my continued participation. Life may, indeed, go on – but I am aware of no compelling argument that I am morally obligated to "go on" with it. Socrates departed voluntarily – as did Cato. They are not villains for having done so. They maintained their integrity. They chose death before dishonor. Would that more of us could exhibit similar fortitude. Let us not dishonor ourselves if we can help it.

References

Adams, Robert M. (1973) "A Modified Divine Command Theory of Ethical Wrongness." In *Religion and Morality: A Collection of Essays* (Gene Outka and John P. Reeder, Jr., eds.). Garden City, NY: Anchor Books, pp. 318–347.

Alston, William (1990) "Some Suggestions for Divine Command Theorists." In *Christian Theism and the Problems of Philosophy*. Edited by Michael Beaty. Notre Dame, IN: University of Notre Dame Press, pp. 303–326.

Barrow, John and Tipler, Frank (1986) *The Anthropic Cosmological Principle*. Clarendon Press.

Becker, L. (1998) *A New Stoicism*. Princeton, NJ: Princeton University Press.

Berlinski, David (2009) *The Devil's Delusion: Atheism and Its Scientific Pretensions*. New York: Crown Forum.

Bobzien, S. (1998) *Determinism and Freedom in Stoic Philosophy*. Oxford: Clarendon Press.

Bodhi, Bhikkhu (trans.) (2005) *In the Buddha's Words: An Anthology of Discourses from the Pali Canon*. Somerville, MA: Wisdom Publications, Inc.

Botros, S. (1985) "Freedom, Causality, Fatalism and Early Stoic Philosophy." *Phronesis* 30, pp. 274–304.

Bourne, E. and Garano, L. (2003) *Coping with Anxiety: 10 Simple Ways to Relieve Anxiety, Fear & Worry*. Oakland, CA: New Harbinger Publications, Inc.

Brandt, Richard (1975) "A Moral Principle about Killing" in Marvin Kohl (ed.), *Beneficent Euthanasia* (Amherst, NY: Prometheus Books). Reprinted in *Ethics: Theory and Contemporary Issues* (4th Ed.), Barbara MacKinnon (ed.). Belmont, CA: Wadsworth, 2004.

Burns, D. (1989) *The Feeling Good Handbook*. New York: Penguin Books USA, Inc.

Camus, Albert (1958) *The Fall*. New York: Alfred A. Knopf, Inc.

Camus, Albert (1955) *The Myth of Sisyphus and Other Essays*. Justin O'Brien (trans.). New York: Random House, Inc.

Center For Science and Culture. "Bibliographic and Annotated List of Peer-Reviewed Publications Supporting Intelligent Design" (2015): <http://www.discovery.org/scripts/viewDB/filesDB-download.php?command=download&id=10141>

Cicero. *On Fate*. AA Long and DN Sedley (trans.), *The Hellenistic Philosophers*. Volume 1. Cambridge: Cambridge University Press, 1987.

Comte-Sponville, A. (1996) *A Small Treatise on the Great Virtues: The Uses of Philosophy in Everyday Life*. New York: Henry Holt and Company, LLC.

Craig, William L. (1990) "The Teleological Argument and the Anthropic Principle." In *The Logic of Rational Theism: Exploratory Essays*, pp. 127–153. Edited by Wm. L. Craig and M. McLeod. *Problems in Contemporary Philosophy* 24. Lewiston, NY: Edwin Mellen.

Craig, William Lane. "Critical review of *The Anthropic Cosmological Principle*." *International Philosophical Quarterly* 27 (1987), pp. 437–47.

Craig, William Lane. "Barrow and Tipler on the Anthropic Principle vs. Divine Design." *British Journal for the Philosophy of Science* 38 (1988), pp. 389–395.

Craig, William Lane. "The Existence of God and the Beginning of the Universe." *Truth: A Journal of Modern Thought* 3 (1991), pp. 85–96. <http://www.reasonablefaith.org/the-existence-of-god-and-the-beginning-of-the-universe#ixzz45uqh1HSS>

Davies, Paul (1983) *God and the New Physics*. New York: Simon & Schuster.

Dawkins, Richard (2007) Debate with John Lennox: <http://fixed-point.org/video/35-full-length/164-the-dawkins-lennox-debate>

Dawkins, Richard (2006) *The God Delusion*. Boston, New York:

Houghton Mifflin Company.

Deem, Rich. "Evidence For The Fine Tuning Of The Universe." *God and Science* (2016): <http://www.godandscience.org/apologetics/designun.html>

Dembski, William. *The Design Inference: Eliminating Chance Through Small Probabilities*. In *Cambridge Studies in Probability, Induction, and Decision Theory*. Cambridge: Cambridge University Press, 1998.

Easwaran, Eknath (trans.) (1985) *The Dhammapada*. Chapter introductions by Stephen Ruppenthal. Tomales, California: Nilgiri Press.

Elgin, D. (1993) *Voluntary Simplicity: Toward a Way of Life that is Outwardly Simple, Inwardly Rich*. New York: William Morrow and Company.

Ellis, A. and Harper, R. (1997) *A Guide to Rational Living* (3rd edition). Hollywood, CA: Melvin Powers, Wilshire Book Company.

Epictetus. *Discourses and Enchiridion*. Thomas W. Higginson (trans.) (1944). New York: Walter J. Black, Inc.

Epictetus. Long, G. & Epictetus (1916) *The Discourses of Epictetus: With the Encheiridion and Fragments*. London: G. Bell and Sons.

Epictetus (1980) *The Golden Sayings of Epictetus*. Champaign, IL: Project Gutenberg; Boulder, CO: NetLibrary.

Fackenheim, Emil (1978) *The Jewish Return Into History: Reflections in the Age of Auschwitz and a New Jerusalem*. New York: Schocken Books.

Feldman, Fred (1991) "Some Puzzles About the Evil of Death." *Philosophical Review* 100, no. 2 (April), pp. 205–227.

Flew, Antony (1979) *A Dictionary of Philosophy: Revised Second Edition*. New York: St. Martin's Press.

Gill, NS (2017) "The Suicide of Cato the Younger." *ThoughtCo.* <https://www.thoughtco.com/the-suicide-of-cato-the-younger-117942>

Hadot, P. (1995) *Philosophy As a Way of Life: Spiritual Exercises from*

Socrates to Foucault, trans. Michael Chase. Oxford: Blackwell Publishers.

Halvorson, Hans and Kragh, Helge. "Cosmology and Theology." *Stanford Encyclopedia of Philosophy* (Fall 2013 Edition), Edward N. Zalta (ed.), URL: <http://plato.stanford.edu/archives/fall2013/entries/cosmology-theology/>

Hamilton, Edith & Cairns, Huntington (eds.) (1961) *Plato: The Collected Dialogues*. Princeton, NJ: Princeton University Press.

Harris, Sam (2005) *The End of Faith: Religion, Terror, and the Future of Reason*. New York, London: WW Norton & Company.

Harris, Sam (2010) *The Moral Landscape: How Science Can Determine Human Values*. New York: Free Press (a division of Simon & Schuster, Inc.).

Hawking, Stephen (1988) *A Brief History of Time: From the Big Bang to Black Holes*. New York: Bantam Books.

Hawking, Stephen and Mlodinow, Leonard (2010) *The Grand Design*. New York: Bantam Books.

Hick, John (1963) *Philosophy of Religion*. Englewood Cliffs, NJ: Prentice-Hall, Inc.

Hilbert, David. "On the infinite." In *Philosophy of Mathematics: Selected Readings* (Benacerraf, Paul, and Hilary Putnam, eds.). Englewood Cliffs, NJ: Prentice-Hall, 1964.

Hitchens, Christopher (2007) *god is not Great: How Religion Poisons Everything*. New York: Twelve, Hachette Book Group USA.

Holt, Jim (2013) *Why Does the World Exist?: An Existential Detective Story*. London: Profile Books Ltd.

Holy Bible: New International Version (2011) Grand Rapids, MI: Zondervan.

Internet Encyclopedia of Philosophy: <http://www.iep.utm.edu/divine-c/#SH4a>

Irvine, W. (2009) *A Guide to the Good Life: The Ancient Art of Stoic Joy*. Oxford University Press.

Irvine, William (2006) *On Desire: Why We Want What We Want*. New York: Oxford University Press.

Jacoby, Susan (2004) *Freethinkers: A History of American Secularism.* New York: Owl Books, Henry Holt and Company, LLC.

Johnson, BC (1981) *Atheist Debater's Handbook.* Amherst, NY: Prometheus Books.

Kaufmann, Walter (1961) *The Faith of a Heretic.* Garden City, NY: Doubleday & Company, Inc.

Kohl, Marvin (2001) "Wisdom and the Axiom of Futility." *The Philosophical Forum* 32, pp. 73–93.

Kraay, Klaas (2015) *God and the Multiverse: Scientific, Philosophical, and Theological Perspectives.* New York: Routledge.

Long, A. (ed.) (1971) *Problems in Stoicism.* London: Athlone Press, University of London.

Lovell, S. "God as the Grounding of Moral Objectivity: Defending Against the *Euthyphro*." <http://www.helpmewithbiblestudy.org/9system_ethics/print/dc2_euthyphro.pdf>

Marcus Aurelius (1964) *Meditations.* Maxwell Staniforth (trans.). New York: Penguin Books Ltd.

Marquis, Don (1989) "Why Abortion Is Immoral." *The Journal of Philosophy*, vol. LXXXVI, no. 4 (April), pp. 183–202.

Morrison, Robert (Dharmachāri Sāgaramati) (2008) "Three Cheers for Taṇhā." *Western Buddhist Review*: <http://www.westernbuddhistreview.com/vol2/tanha.html>

Morriston, Wes (2009) "What if God commanded something terrible? A worry for divine-command meta-ethics." *Religious Studies* 45, pp. 249–267.

Murphy, MC (2011) *God and Moral Law: On the Theistic Explanation of Morality.* Oxford University Press.

Nagel, Thomas (1970) "Death." *Nous* 4, p. 73.

NIHM (2009) <http://www.nimh.nih.gov/health/publications/anxiety-disorders/introduction.shtml>

Nietzsche, Friedrich (1989) *On the Genealogy of Morals and Ecce Homo.* Walter Kaufmann (trans.). New York: Vintage Books.

Novak, Philip (1995) *The World's Wisdom: Sacred Texts of the World's Religions.* New York: Harper Collins.

Penrose, Roger (1989) *The Emperor's New Mind: Concerning Computers, Minds, and the Laws of Physics*. Oxford: Oxford University Press.

Pigliucci, Massimo (2016) "Epictetus on suicide: the open door policy." *How to Be a Stoic*: <https://howtobeastoic.wordpress.com/2016/04/05/epictetus-on-suicide-the-open-door-policy/>

Plantinga, Alvin. "The Dawkins Confusion: *Naturalism* ad absurdum." *Christianity Today* (March/April 2007).

Plutarch (1919) *Parallel Lives, Volume VIII*. Loeb Classical Library.

Quinn, Philip L. (2006) *Essays in the Philosophy of Religion*. New York: Oxford University Press.

Rahula, W. (1959) *What the Buddha Taught*. New York: Grove Weidenfeld.

Rees, Martin (1998) *Before the Beginning: Our Universe and Others*. New York: Basic Books.

Rescher, Nicholas (1987) *Ethical Idealism: An Inquiry into the Nature and Function of Ideals*. Berkeley: University of California Press.

Robertson, D. (2010) *The Philosophy of Cognitive-Behavioural Therapy (CBT): Stoic Philosophy as Rational and Cognitive Psychotherapy*. London: Karnac Books Ltd.

Sartre, J. (1955) *No Exit and Three Other Plays*. New York: Alfred A. Knopf, Inc.

Searle, John (2004) *Mind: A Brief Introduction*. New York: Oxford University Press.

Seddon, K. (2004) Western Kentucky University Website: <http://www.wku.edu/~jan.garrett/stoa/seddon1.htm>

Sellars, J. (2009) *The Art of Living: The Stoics on the Nature and Function of Philosophy* (2nd Edition). London: Bristol Classical Press.

Seneca (1968) *The Stoic Philosophy of Seneca* (Moses Hadas, trans.). New York: WW Norton & Company, Inc.

Spitzer, Robert (2010) *New Proofs for the Existence of God: Contributions of Contemporary Physics and Philosophy*. Grand Rapids, MI: Wm. B. Eerdmans Publishing Co.

Stenger, Victor (2007) *God – The Failed Hypothesis: How Science Shows That God Does Not Exist*. New York: Prometheus Books.

Sumedho, Ajahn (1991) *The Way It Is*. Hertfordshire, UK: Amaravati Publications.

Taylor, R. (1985) *Ethics, Faith, and Reason*. Englewood Cliffs, NJ: Prentice-Hall.

Thanissaro Bhikkhu (trans.) (1999) *Ājīvaka Sutta*. <http://www.accesstoinsight.org/tipitaka/an/an03/an03.072.than.html>

Thanissaro Bhikkhu (2006) "Desire & Imagination in the Buddhist Path."<http://www.accesstoinsight.org/lib/authors/thanissaro/pushinglimits.html> (revised 08/14/2007).

Vacula, Justin (2017) "Stoicism and Suicide." *Modern Stoicism*: <http://modernstoicism.com/stoicism-and-suicide-by-justin-vacula/>

O-BOOKS

SPIRITUALITY

O is a symbol of the world, of oneness and unity; this eye represents knowledge and insight. We publish titles on general spirituality and living a spiritual life. We aim to inform and help you on your own journey in this life.
If you have enjoyed this book, why not tell other readers by posting a review on your preferred book site?

Recent bestsellers from O-Books are:

Heart of Tantric Sex
Diana Richardson
Revealing Eastern secrets of deep love and intimacy to Western couples.
Paperback: 978-1-90381-637-0 ebook: 978-1-84694-637-0

Crystal Prescriptions
The A-Z guide to over 1,200 symptoms and their healing crystals
Judy Hall
The first in the popular series of six books, this handy little guide is packed as tight as a pill-bottle with crystal remedies for ailments.
Paperback: 978-1-90504-740-6 ebook: 978-1-84694-629-5

365 Days of Wisdom
Daily Messages To Inspire You Through The Year
Dadi Janki
Daily messages which cool the mind, warm the heart and guide
you along your journey.
Paperback: 978-1-84694-863-3 ebook: 978-1-84694-864-0

Body of Wisdom
Women's Spiritual Power and How it Serves
Hilary Hart
Bringing together the dreams and experiences of women across
the world with today's most visionary spiritual teachers.
Paperback: 978-1-78099-696-7 ebook: 978-1-78099-695-0

Practicing A Course In Miracles
A translation of the Workbook in plain language, with
mentor's notes
Elizabeth A. Cronkhite
The practical second and third volumes of The Plain-Language
A Course In Miracles.
Paperback: 978-1-84694-403-1 ebook: 978-1-78099-072-9

Readers of ebooks can buy or view any of these bestsellers by
clicking on the live link in the title. Most titles are published
in paperback and as an ebook. Paperbacks are available in
traditional bookshops. Both print and ebook formats are
available online.
Find more titles and sign up to our readers' newsletter at
http://www.johnhuntpublishing.com/mind-body-spirit
Follow us on Facebook at https://www.facebook.com/OBooks/
and Twitter at https://twitter.com/obooks